Geometric Coloring Books for Adults
A Geometric Mandalas Pattern Coloring Book for Adults

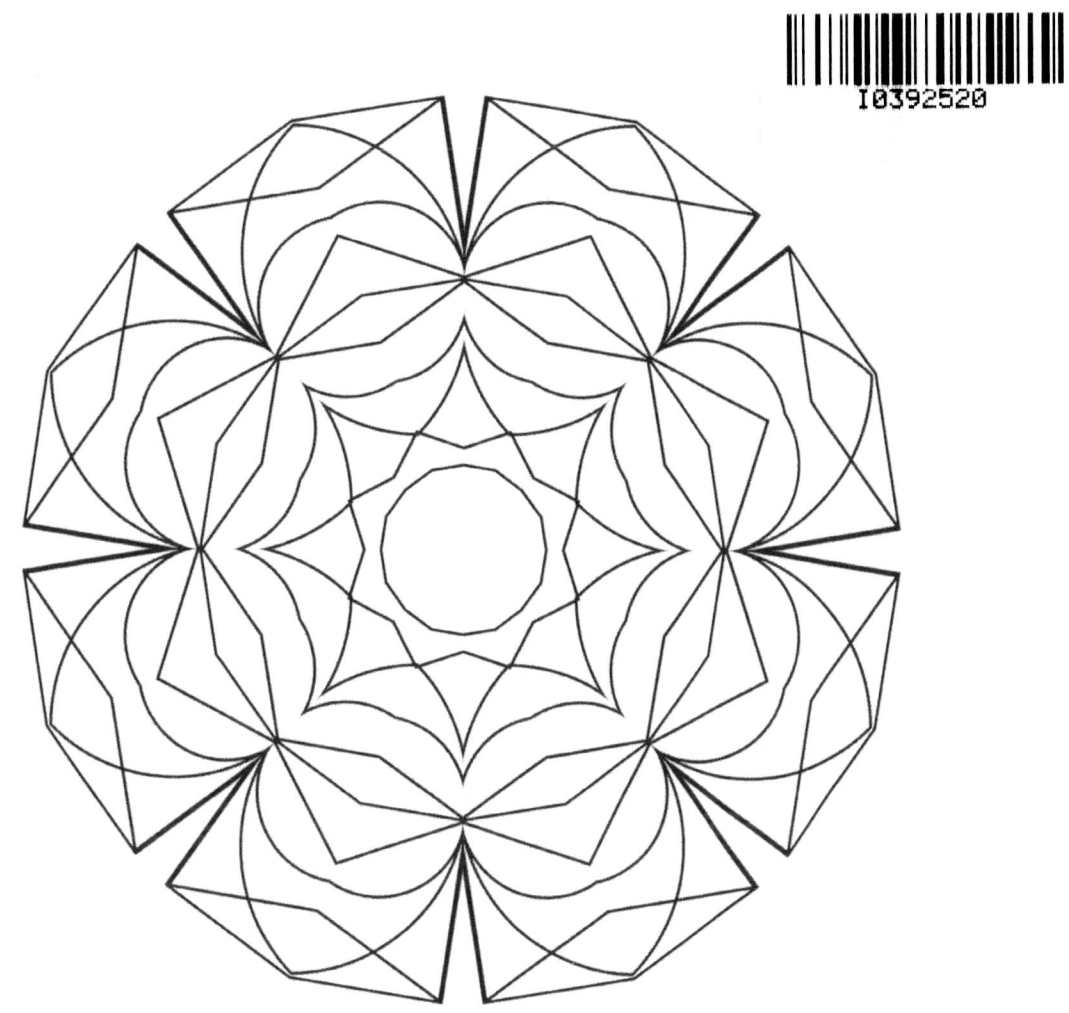

Richard L. Pigg

Geometric Coloring Books for Adults
A Geometric Mandalas Pattern Coloring Book for Adults

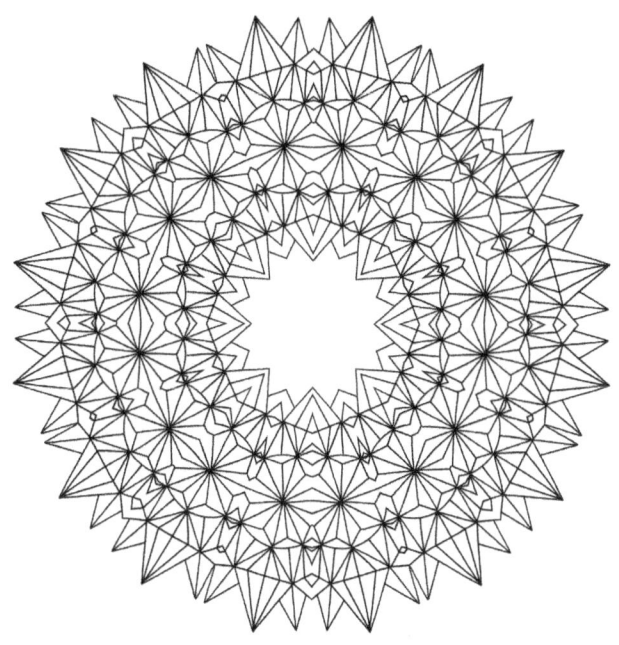

Copyright: Published in the United States by Richard L. Pigg
Published July 2016

All rights reserved. No part of this publication may be reproduced, stored in retrieval system, copied in any form or by any means, electronic, mechanical, photocopying, recording or otherwise transmitted without written permission from the publisher. Please do not participate in or encourage piracy of this material in any way. You must not circulate this book in any format. Richard L. Pigg does not control or direct users' actions and is not responsible for the information or content shared, harm and/or actions of the book readers.

ISBN-13: 978-1535377539

ISBN-10: 1535377534

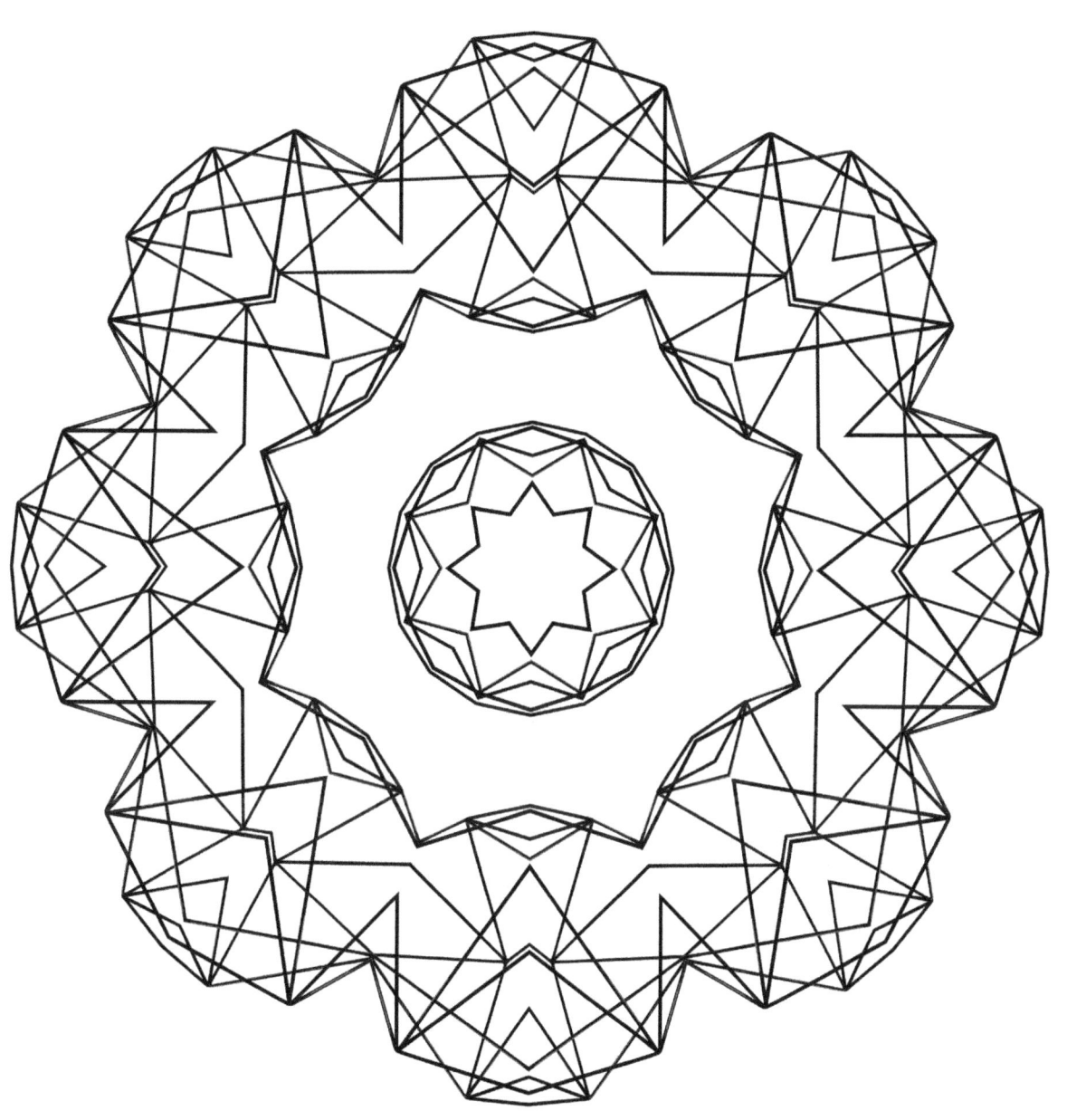

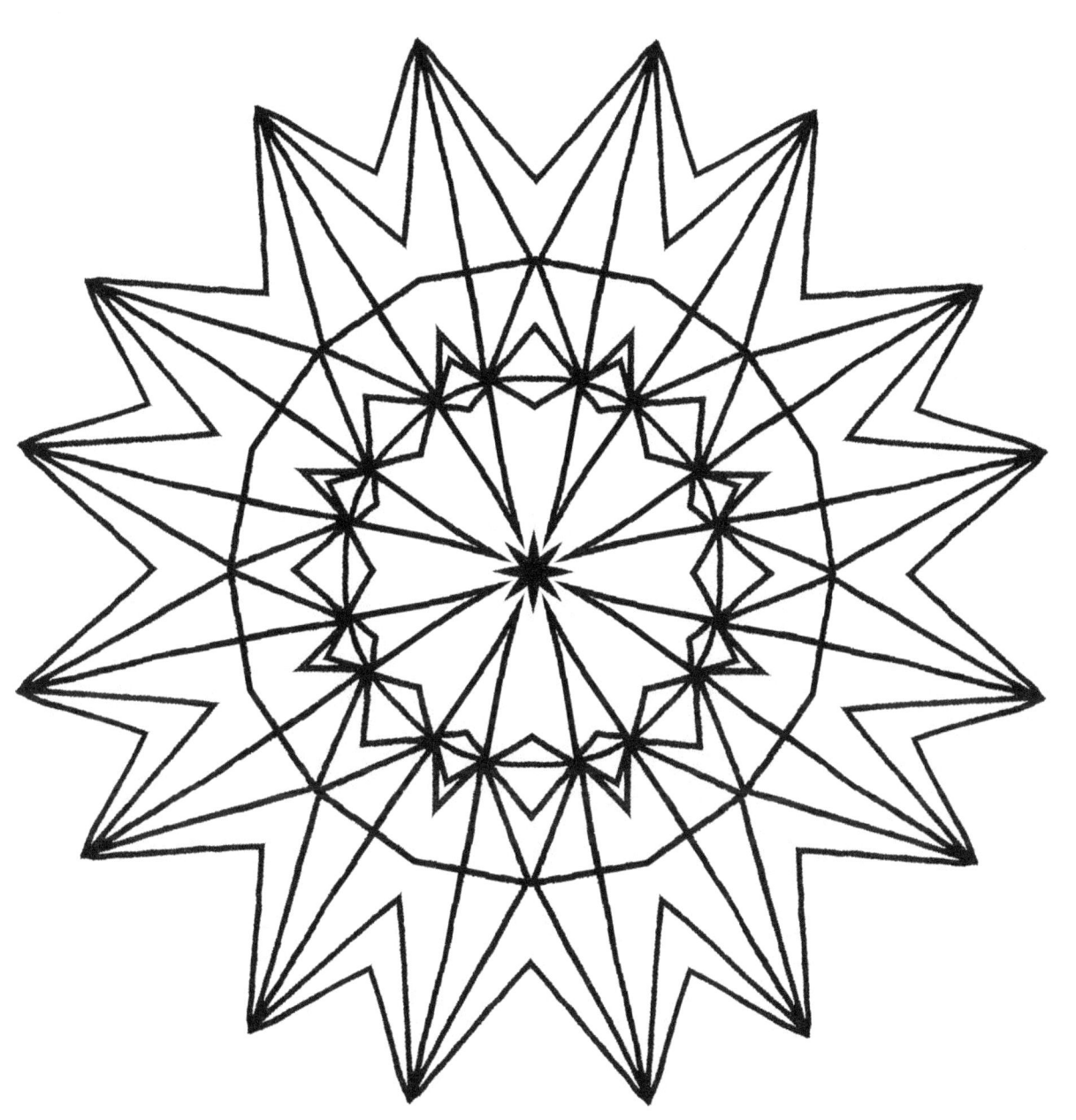

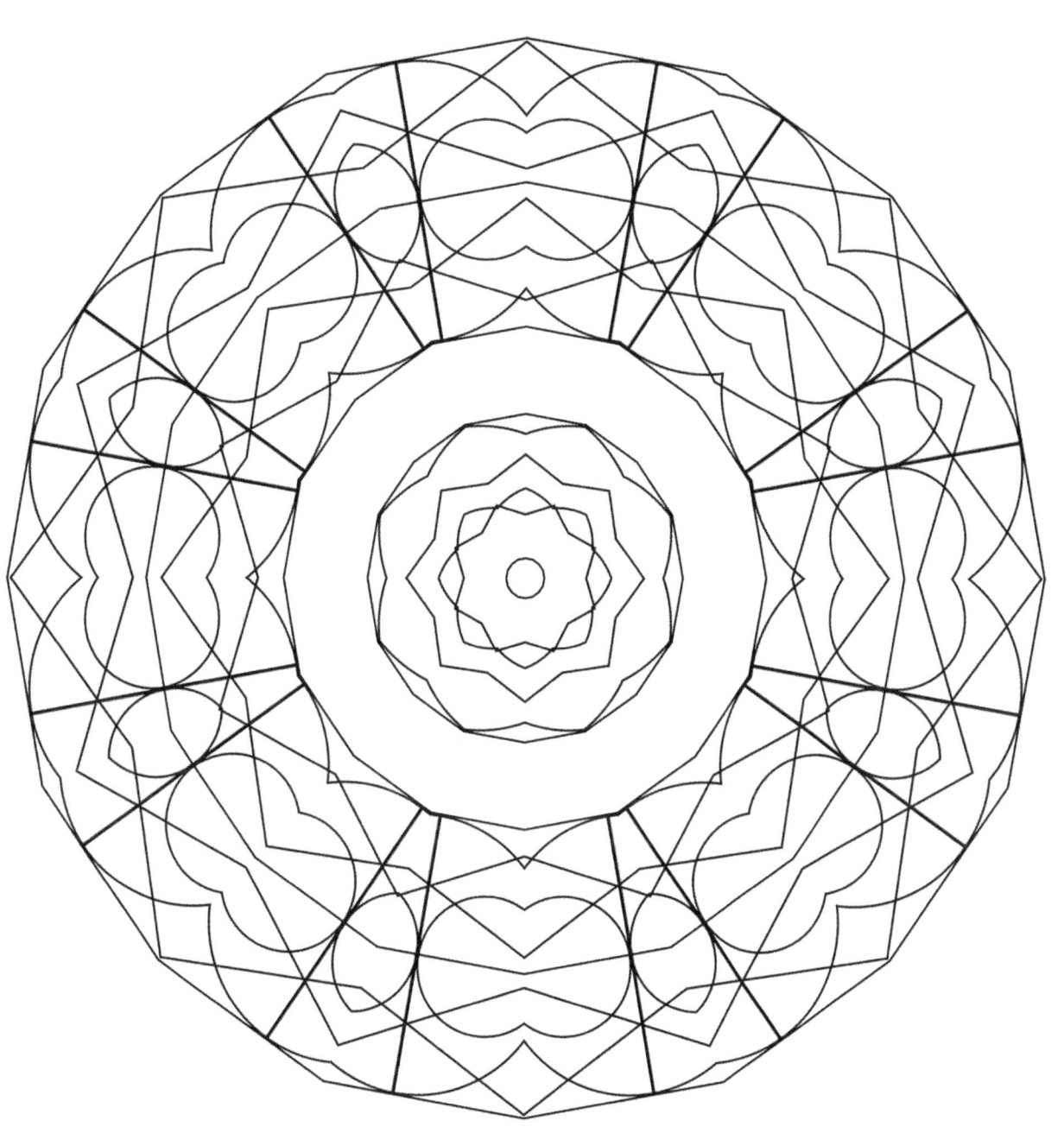

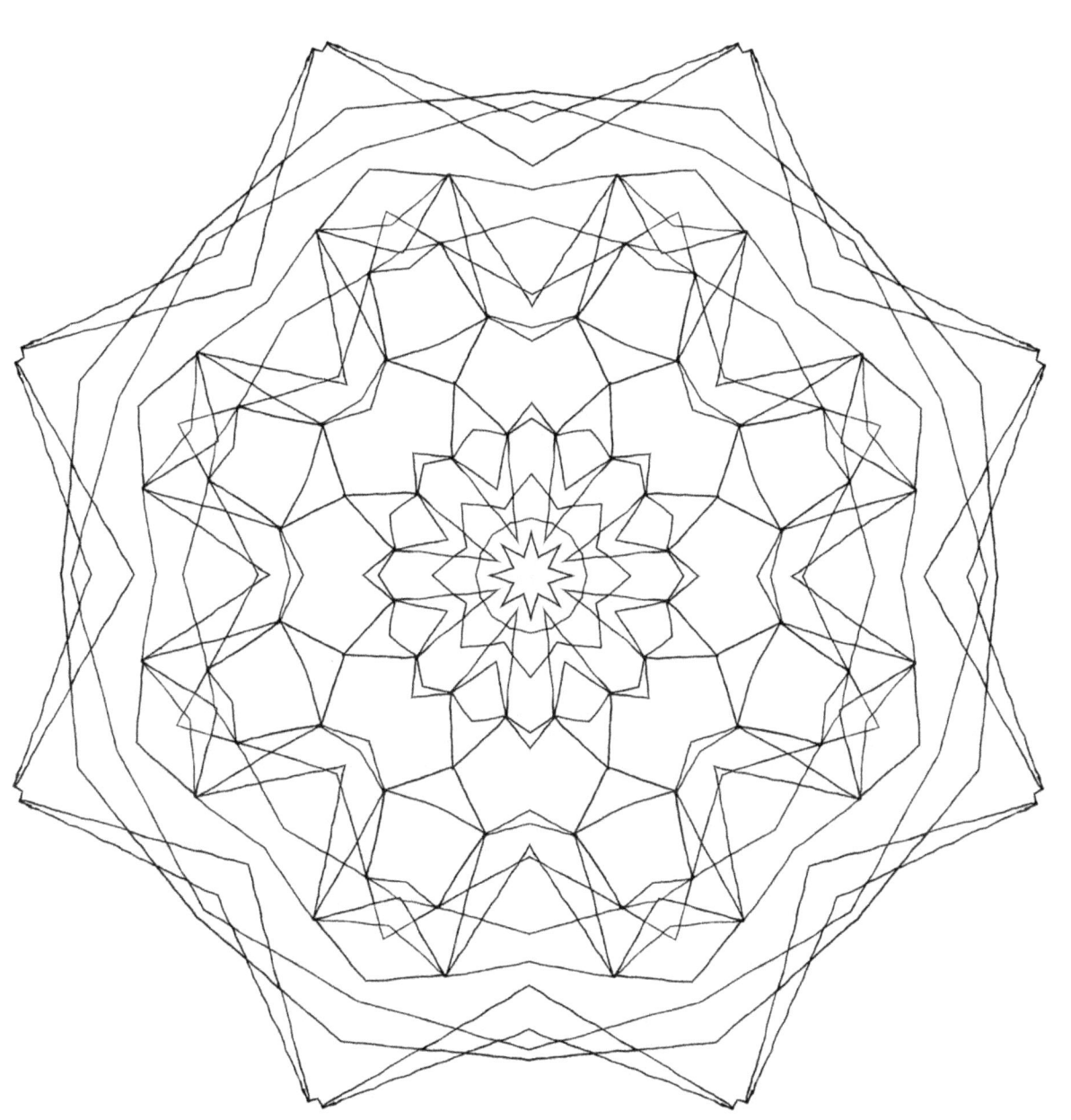

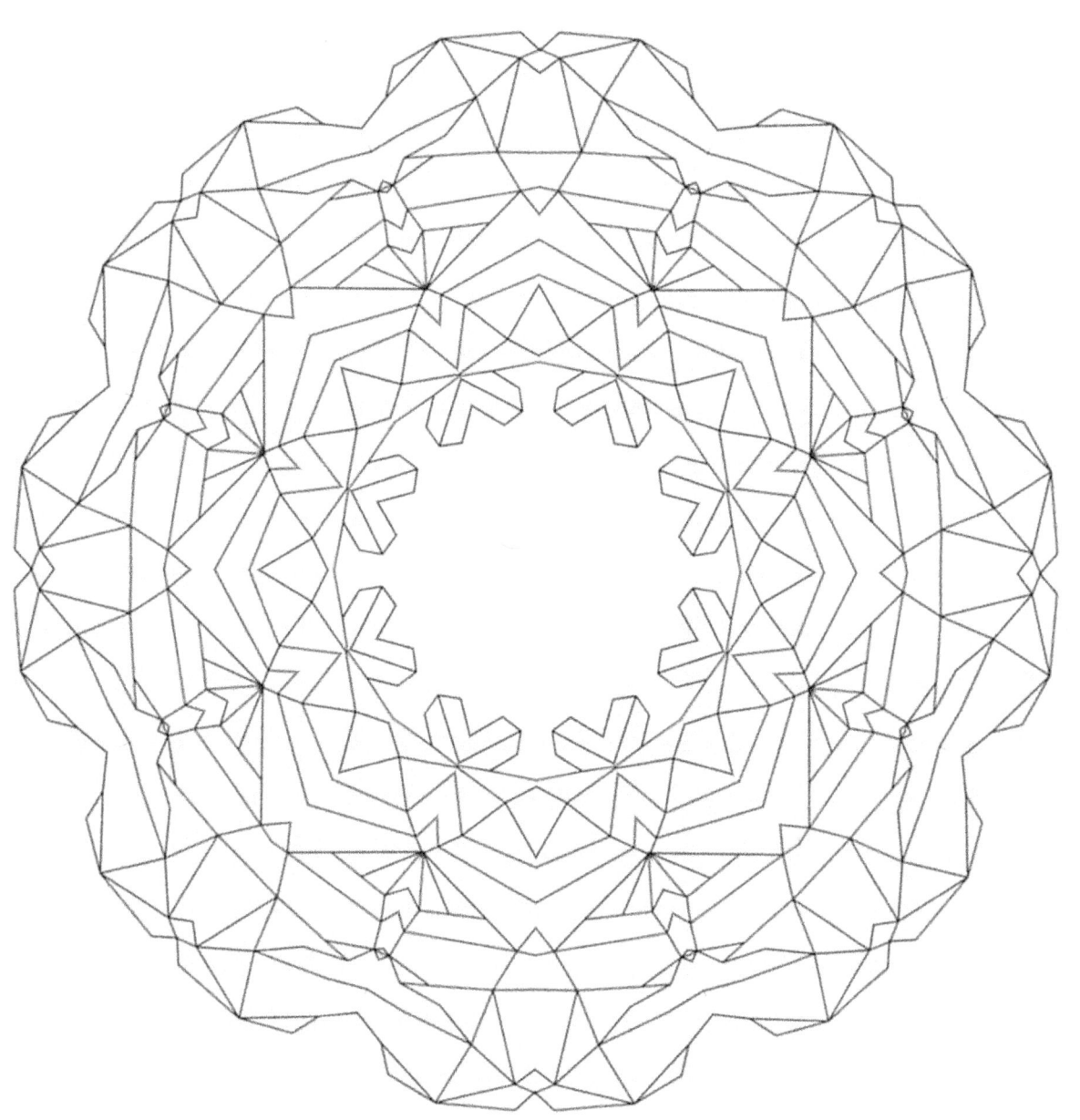

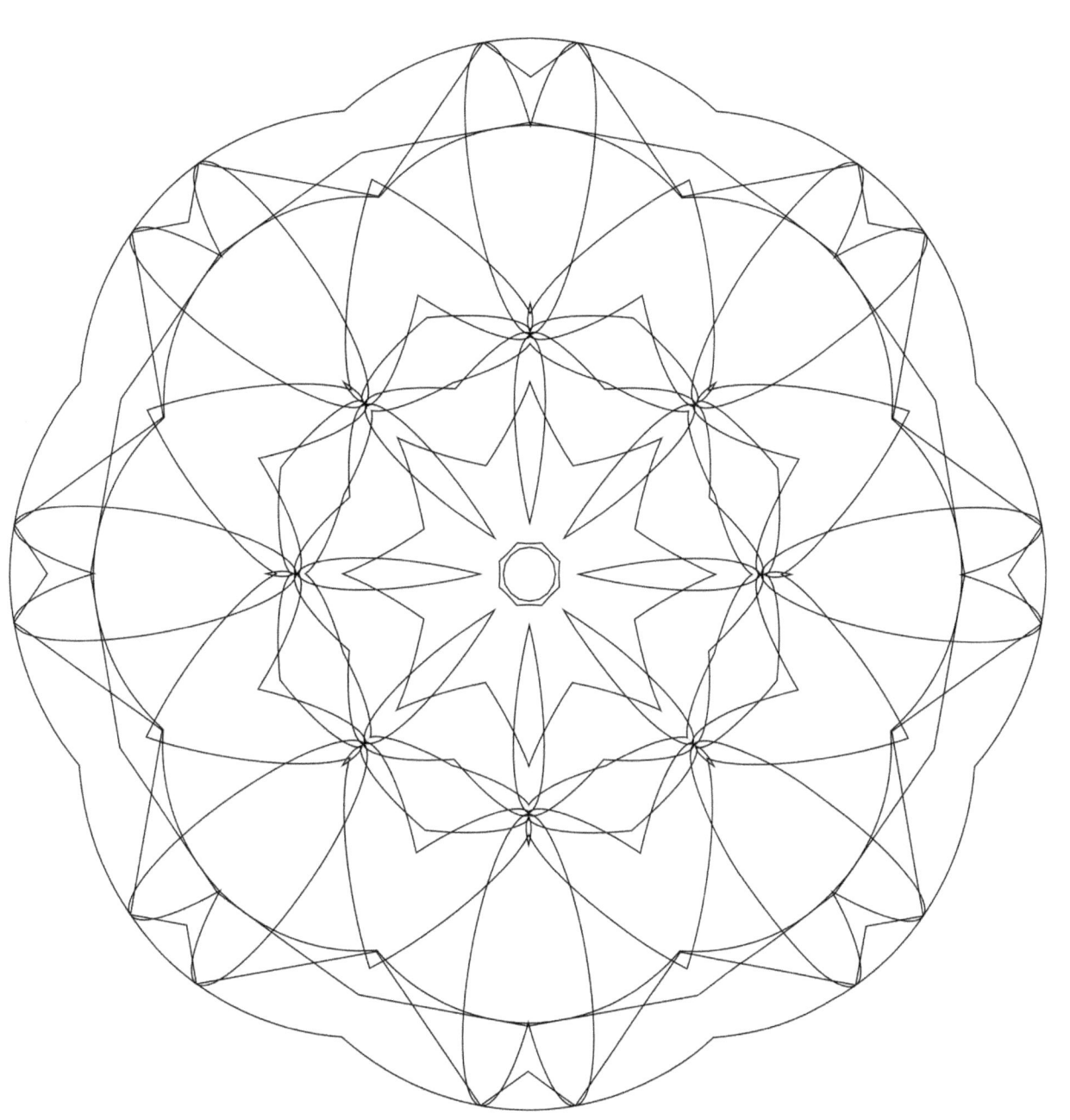

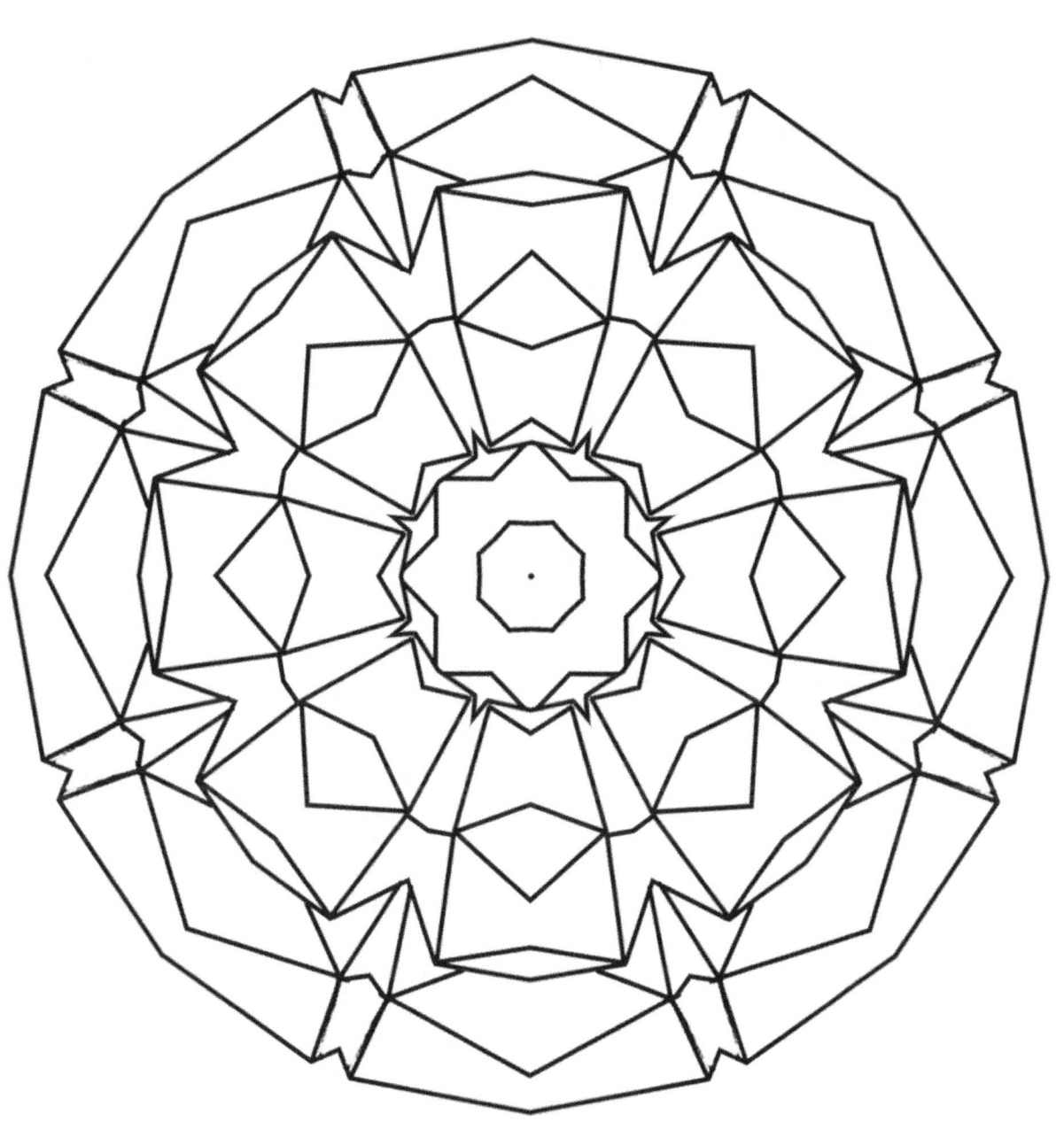

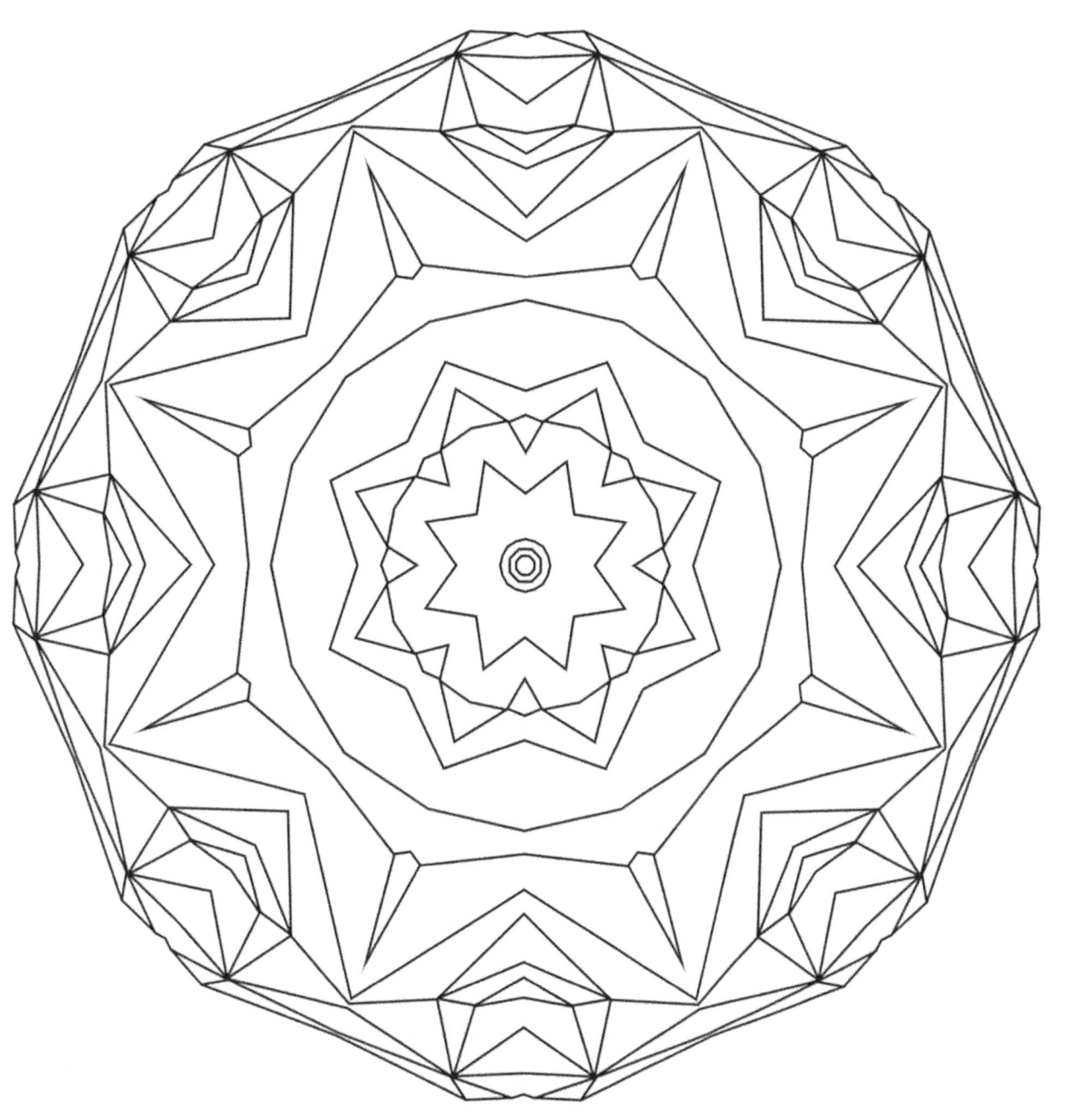

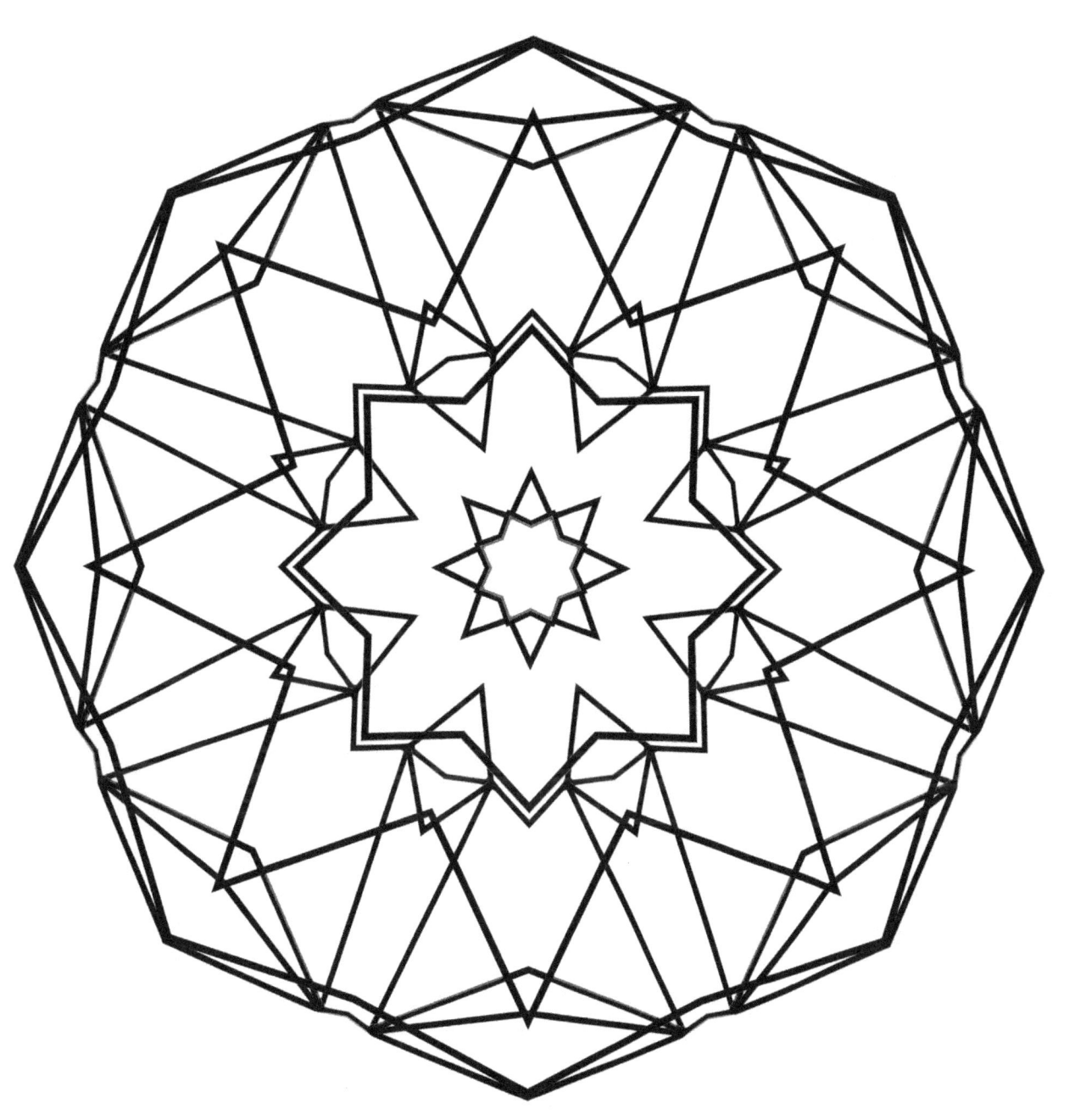

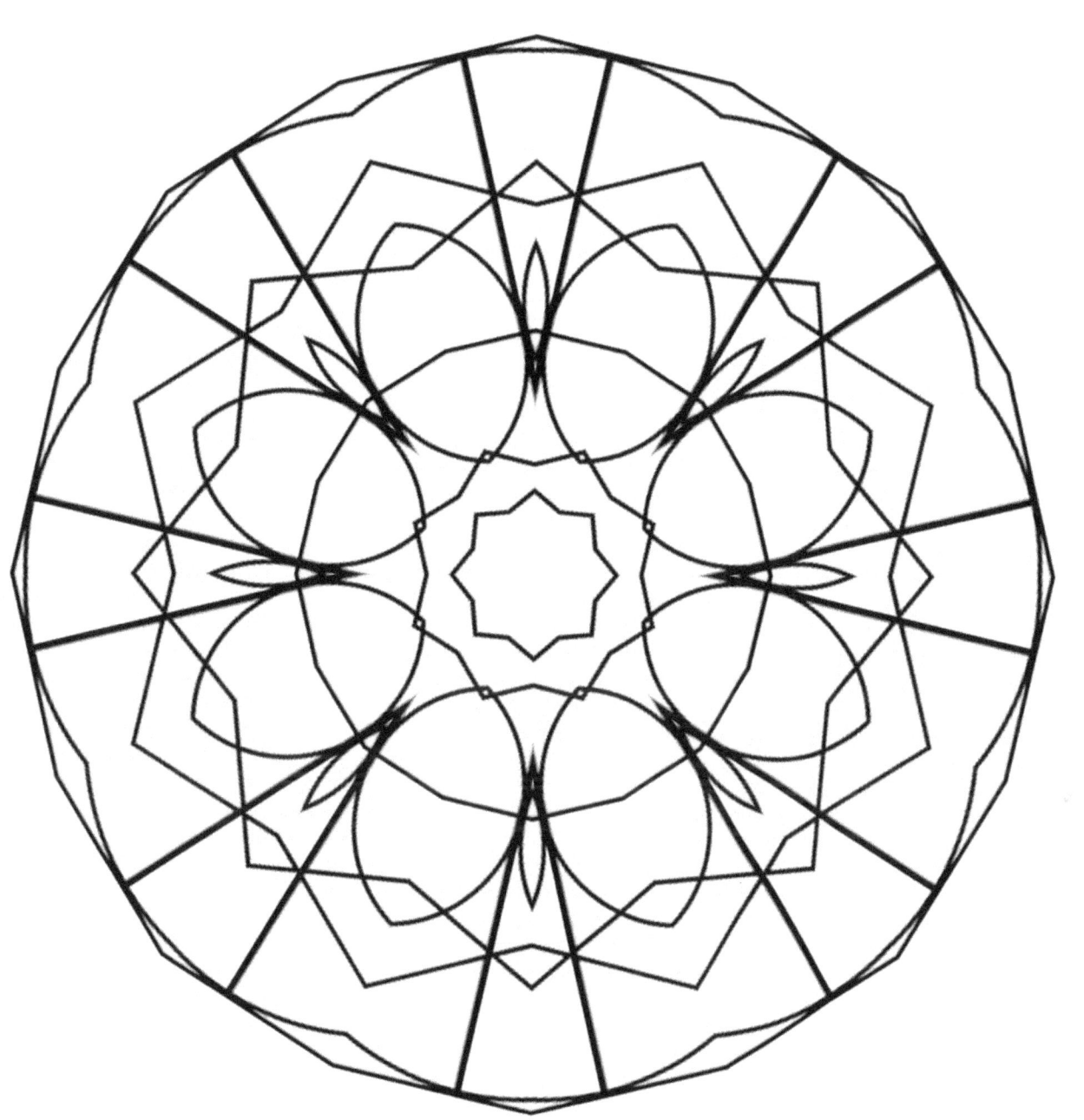

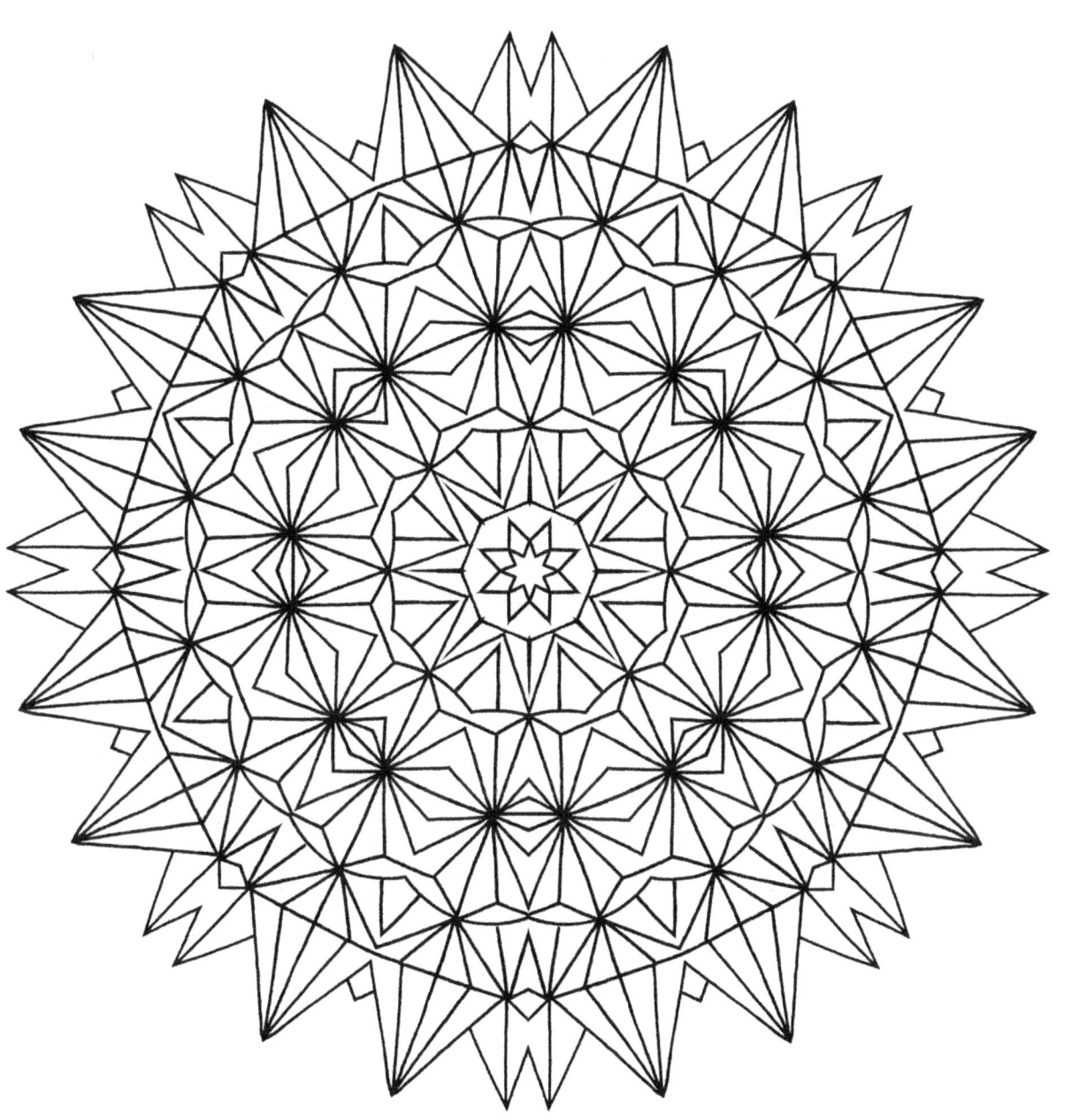

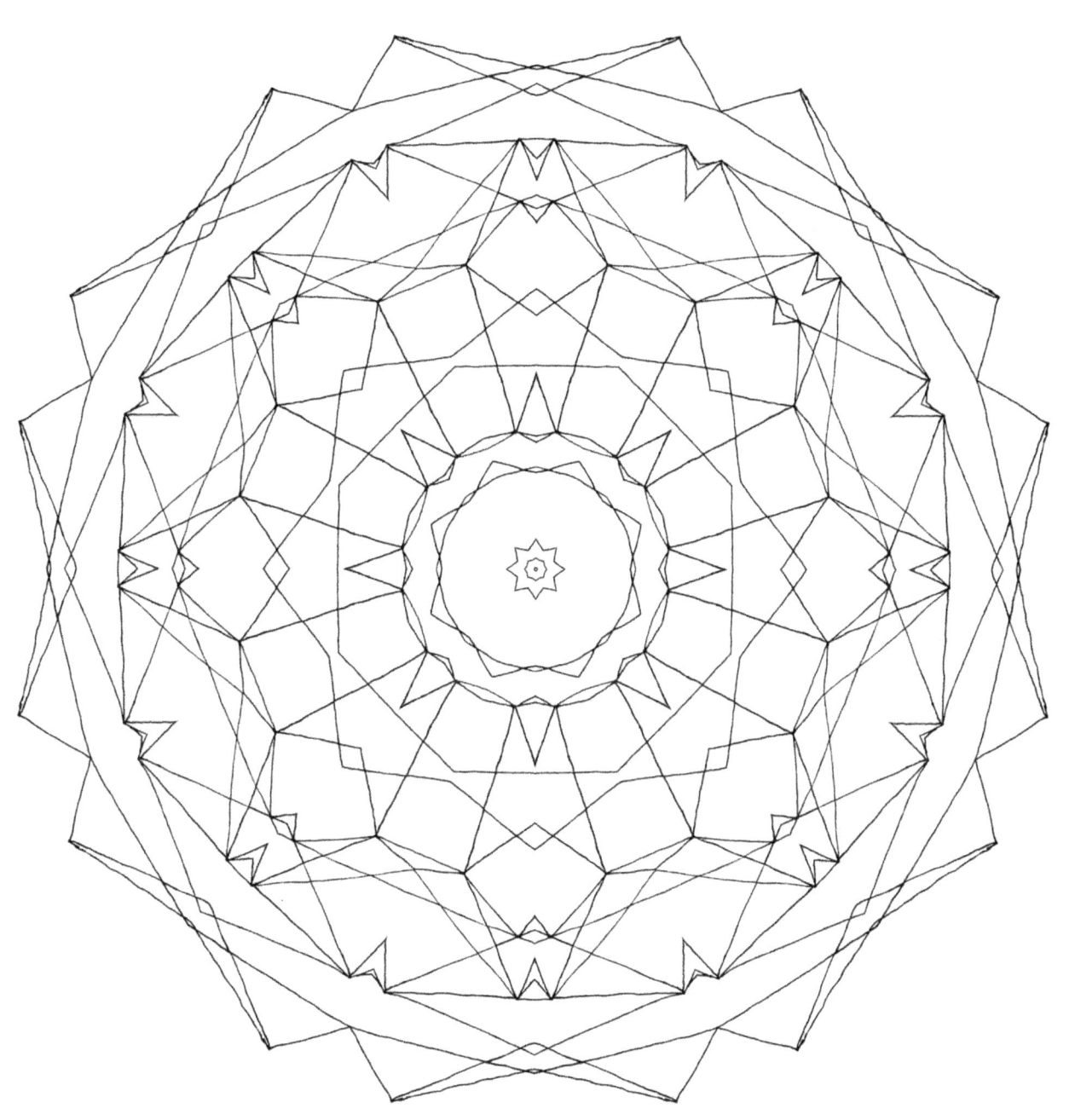

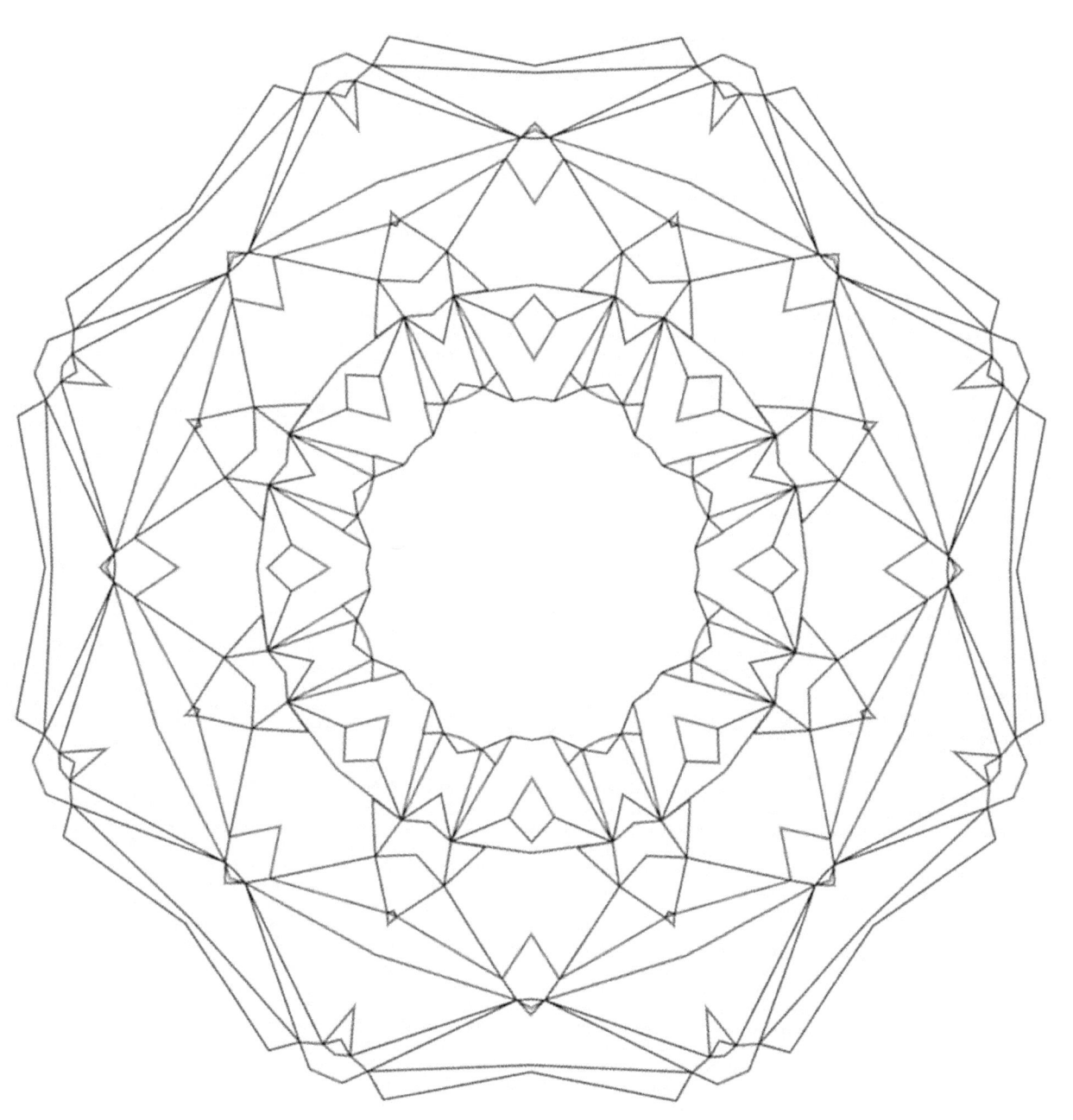

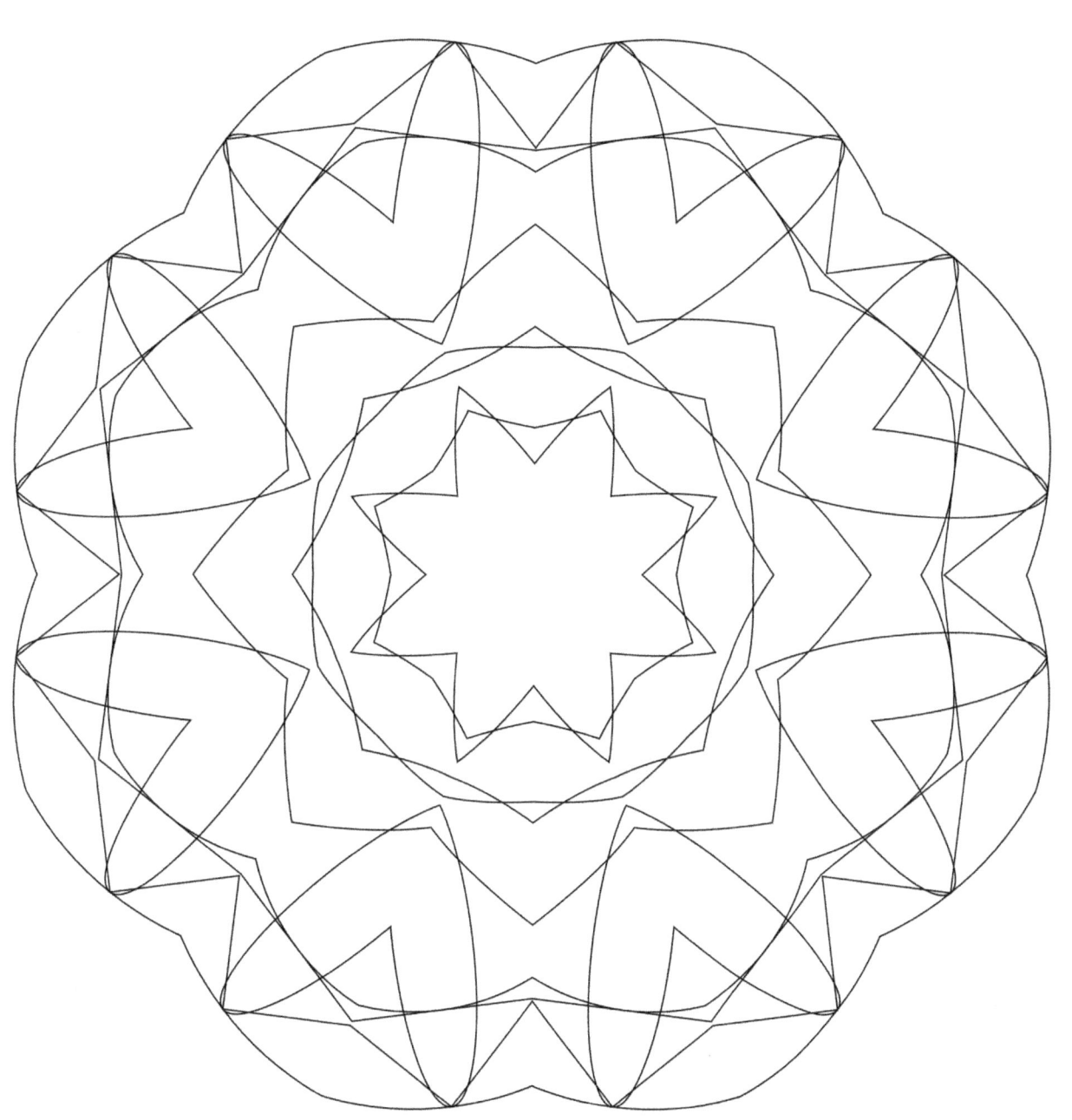

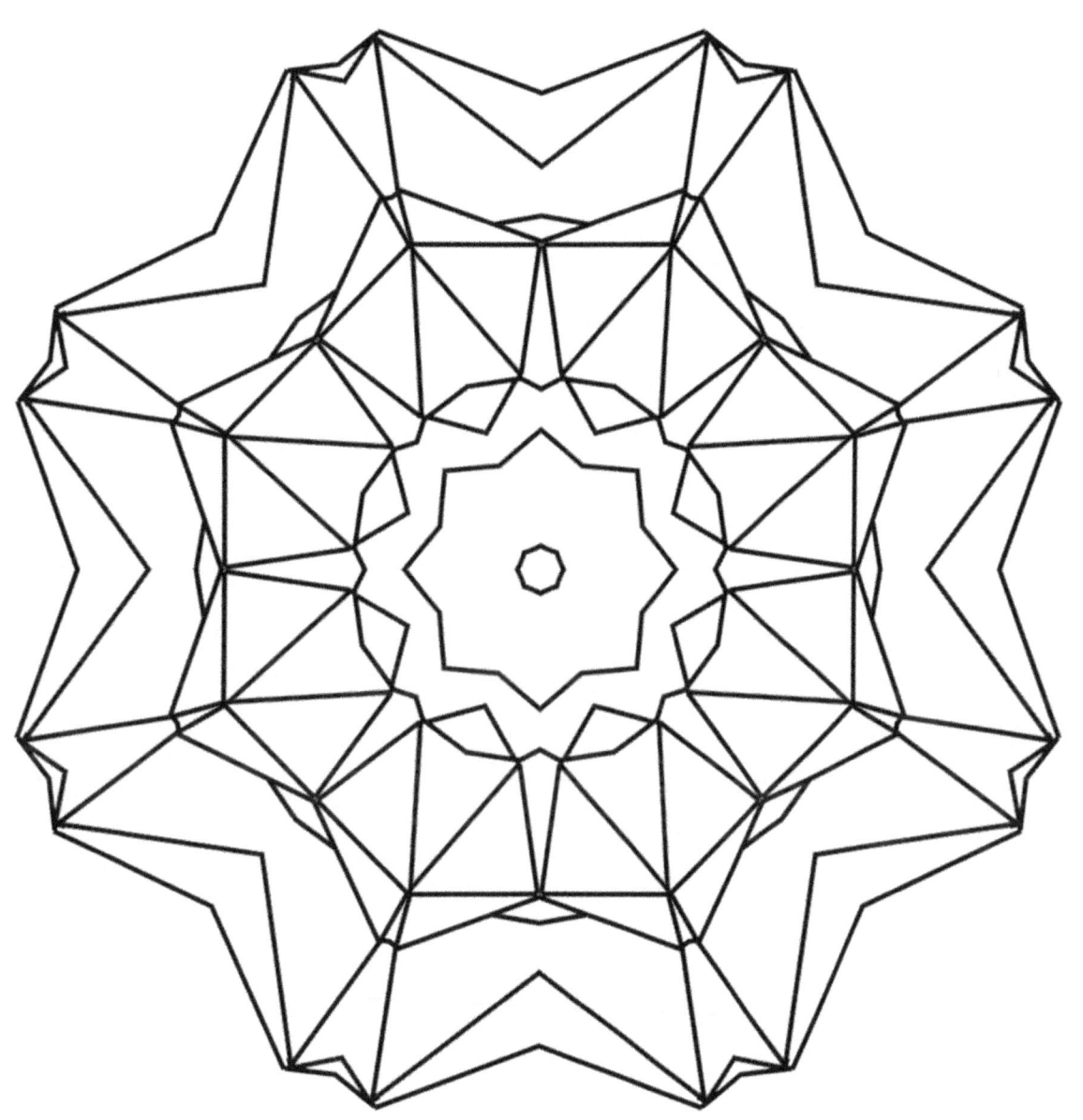

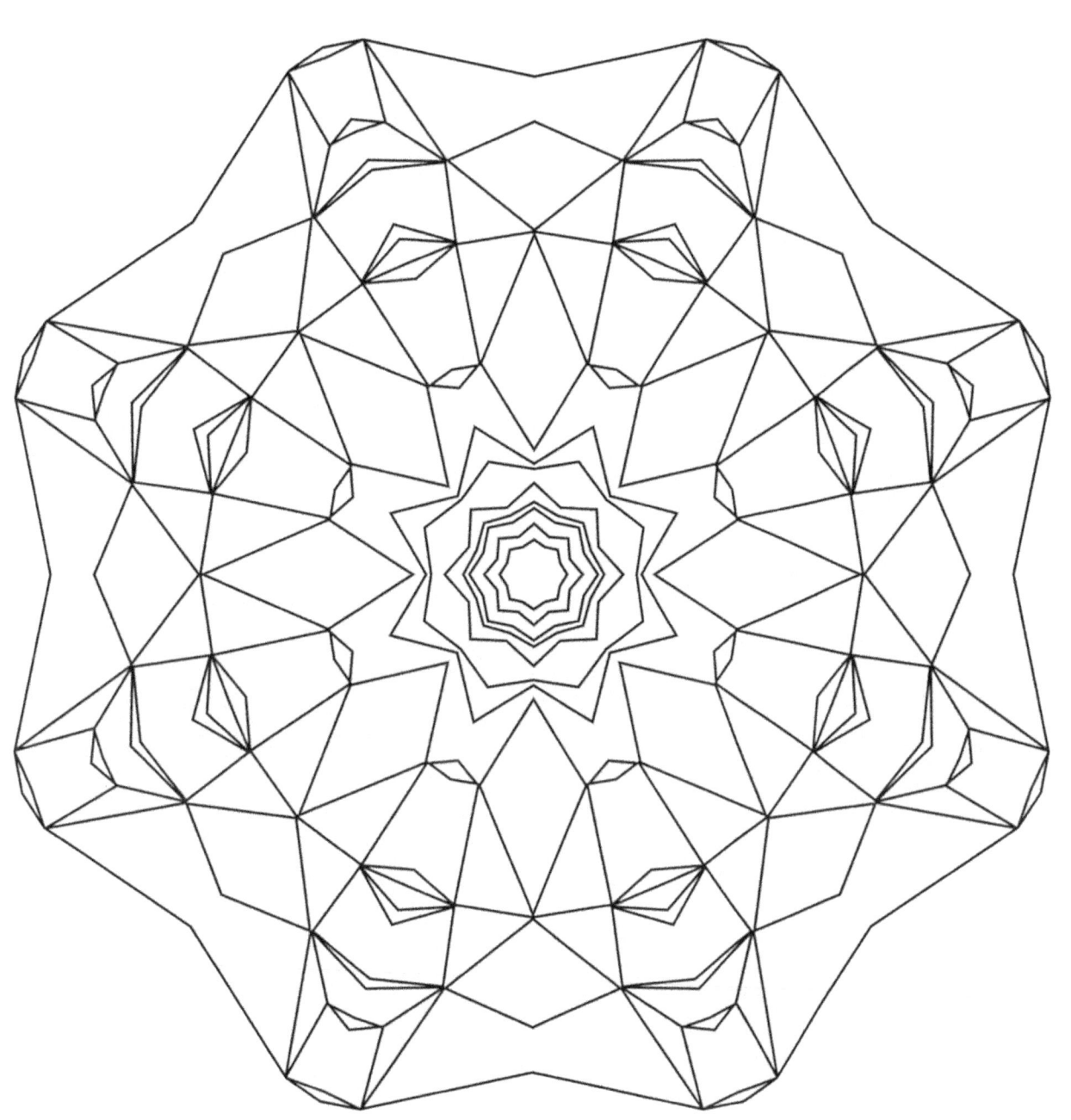

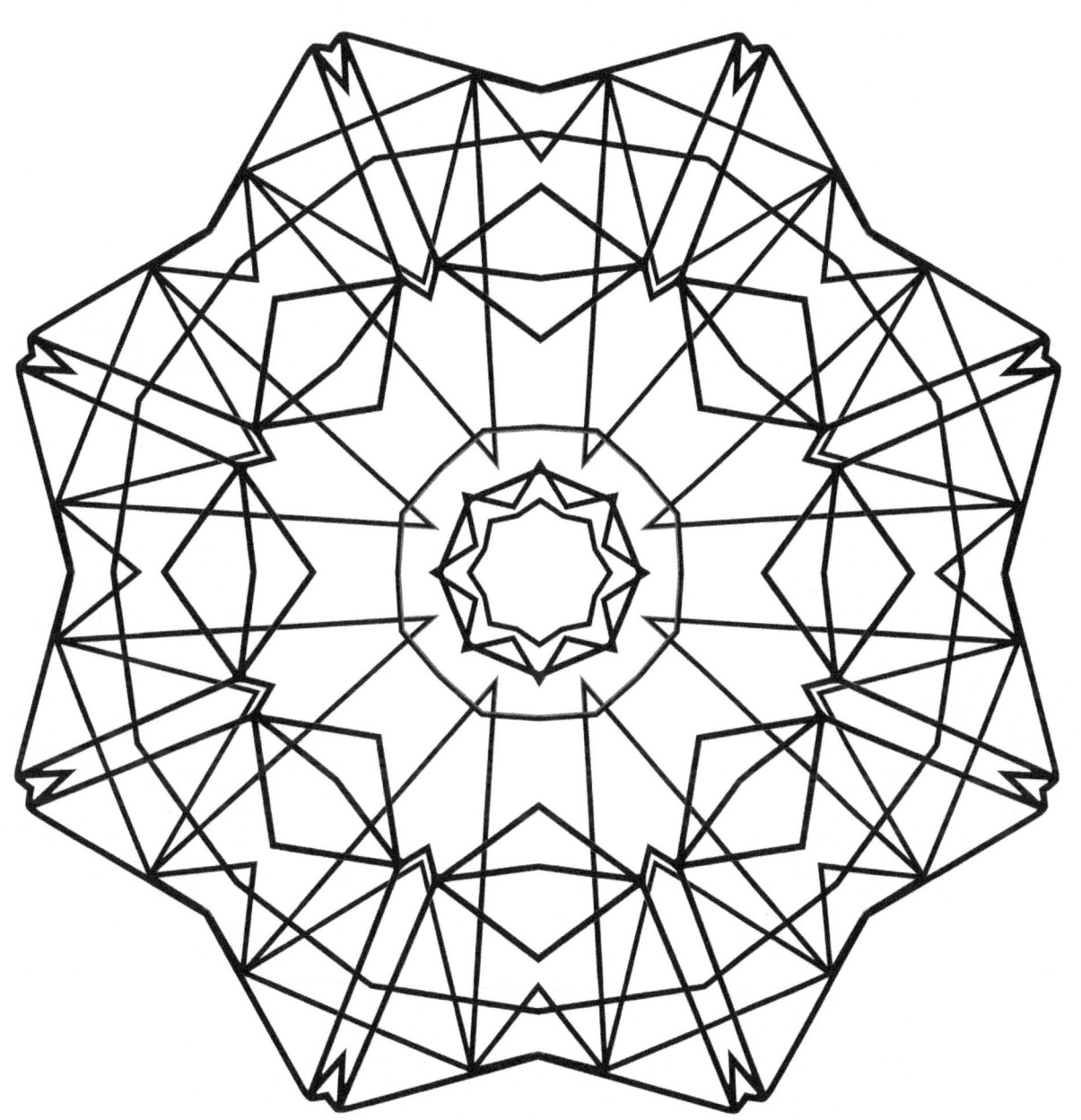

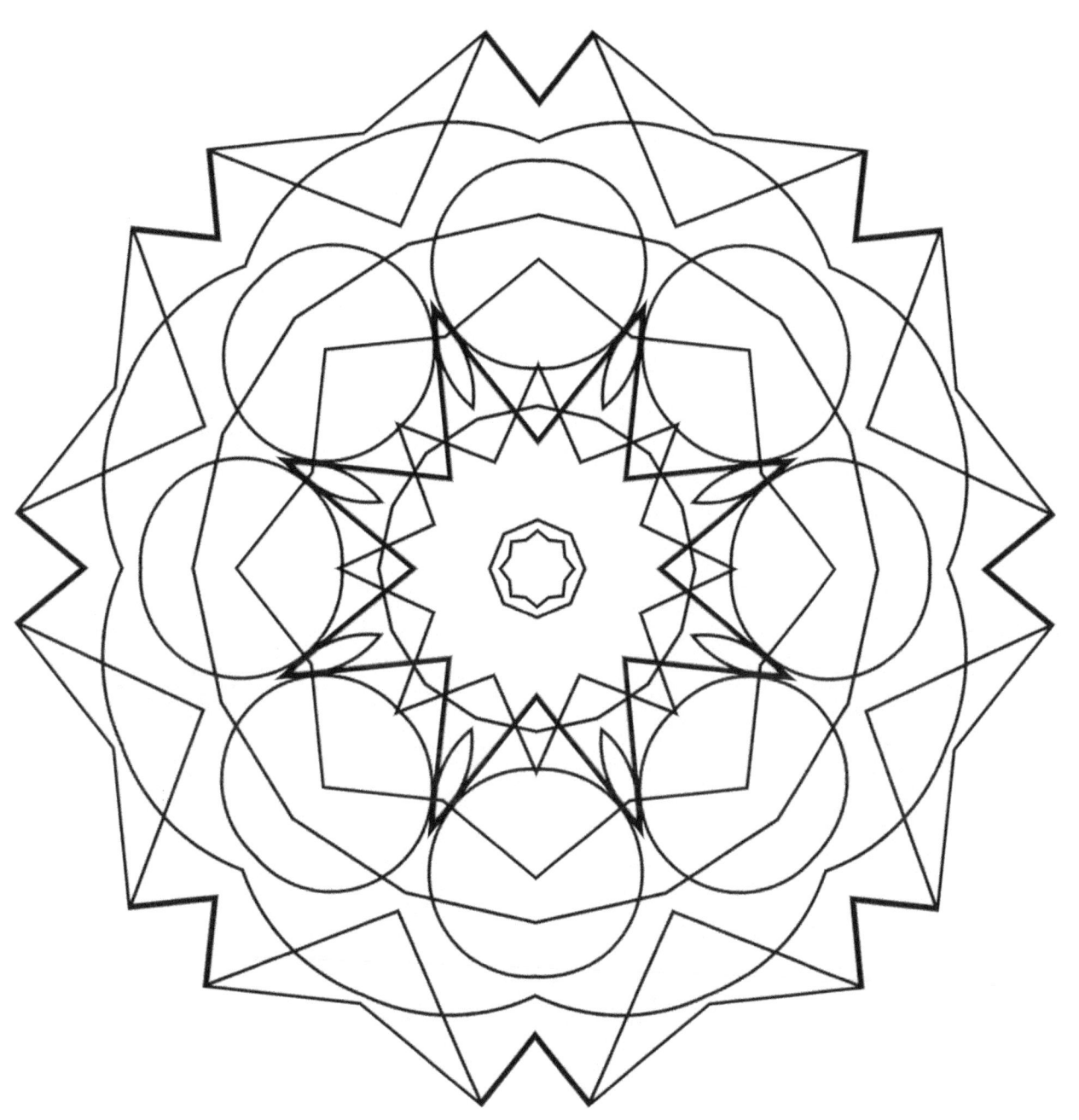

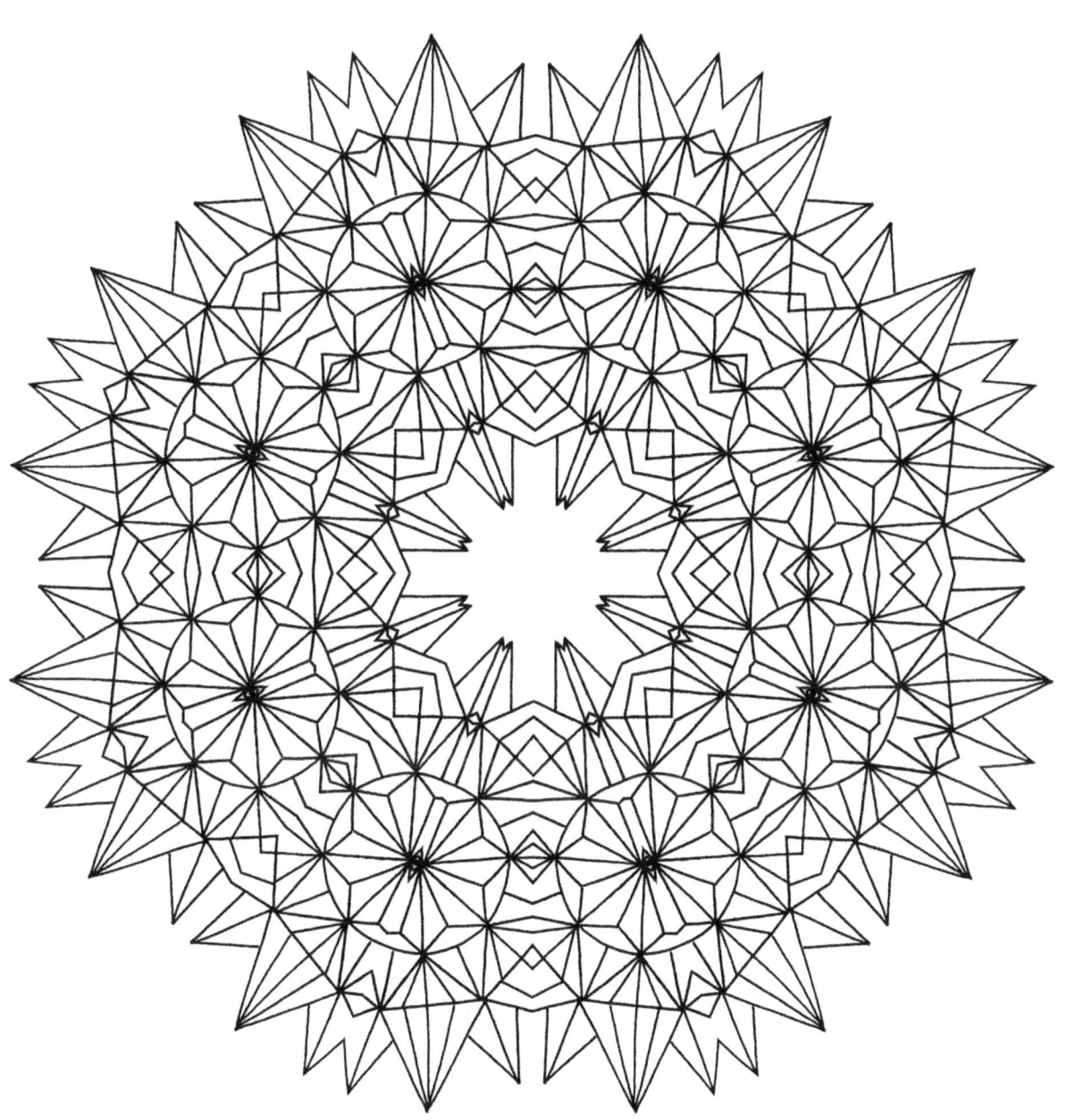

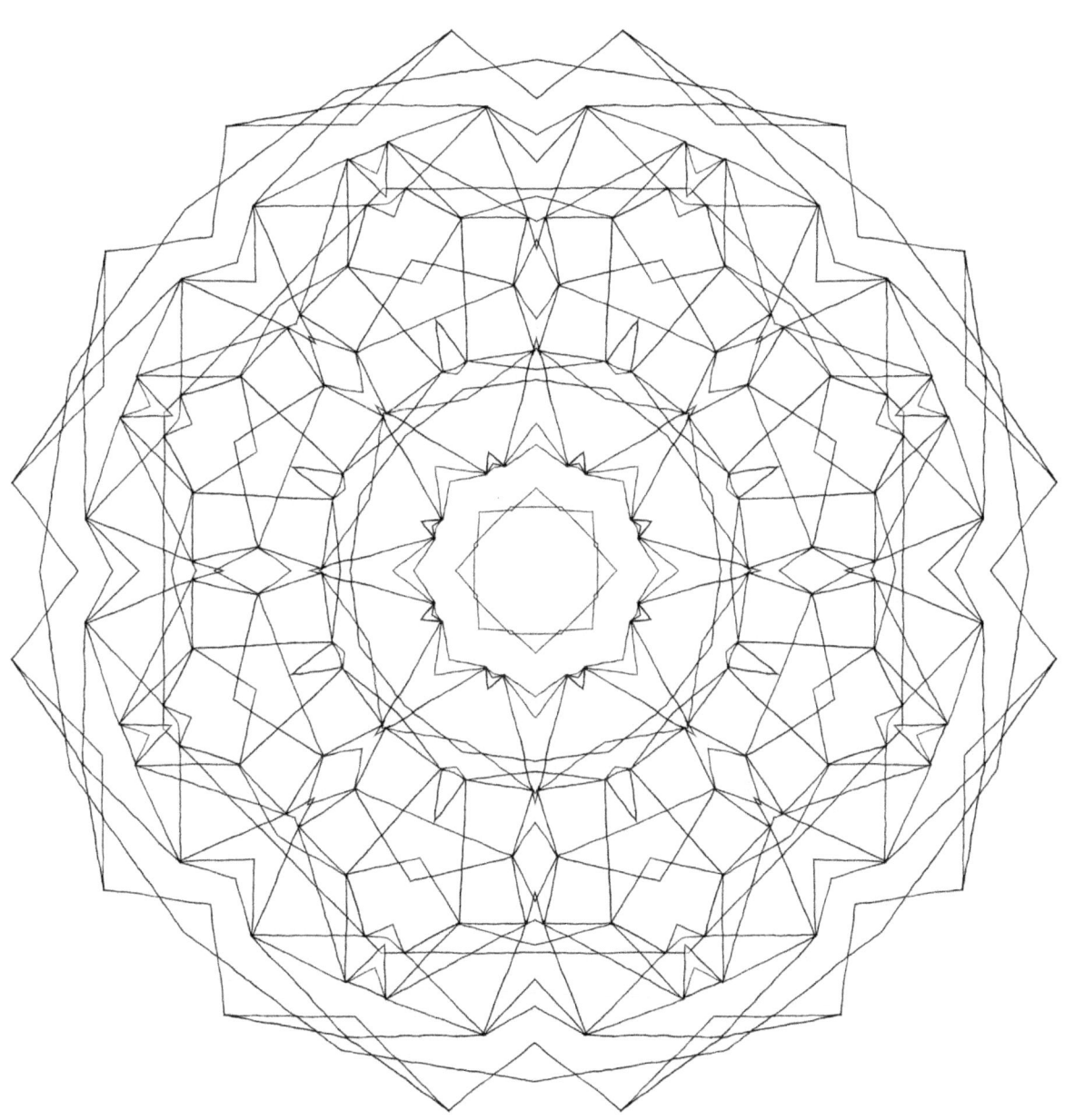

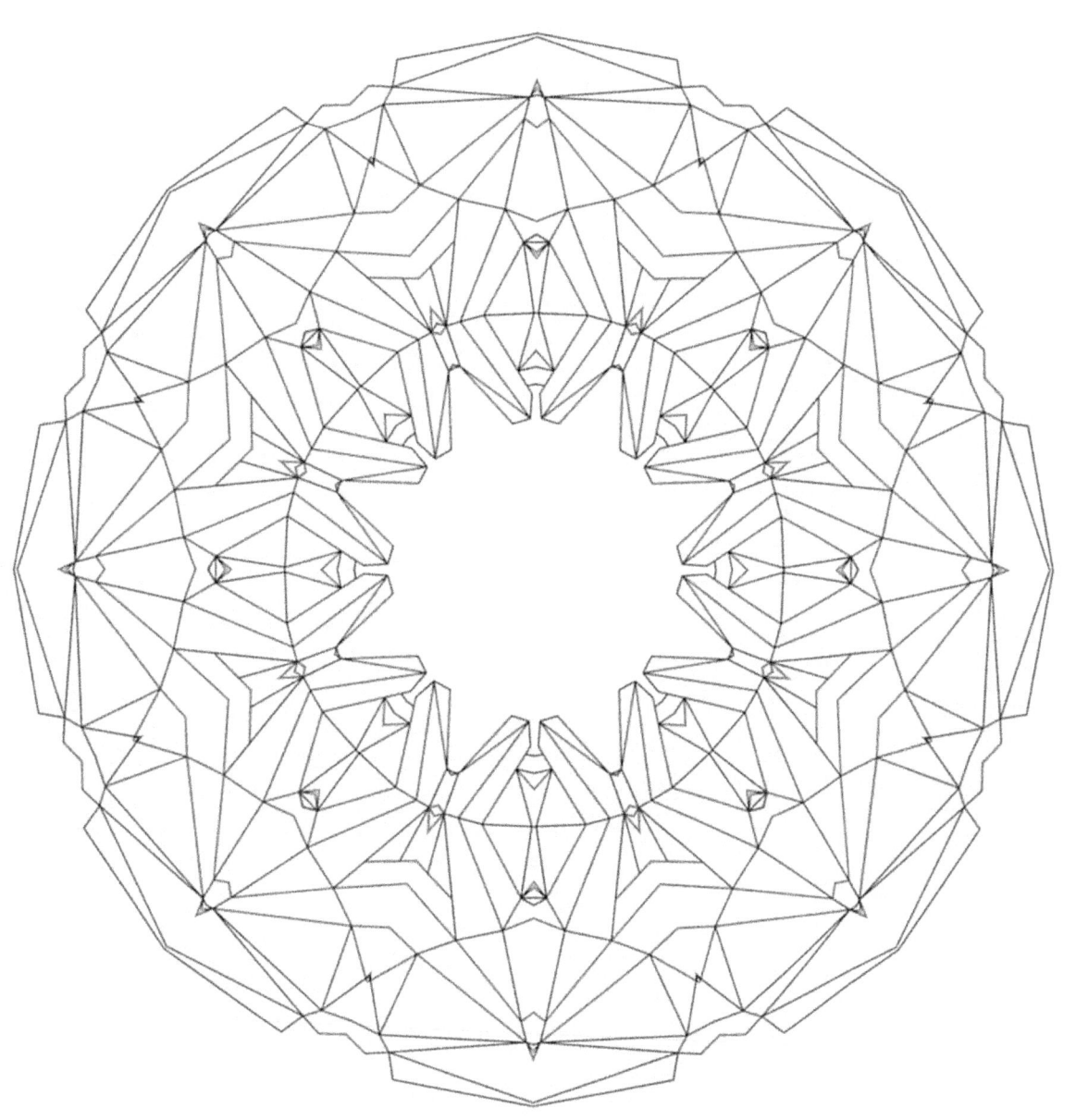

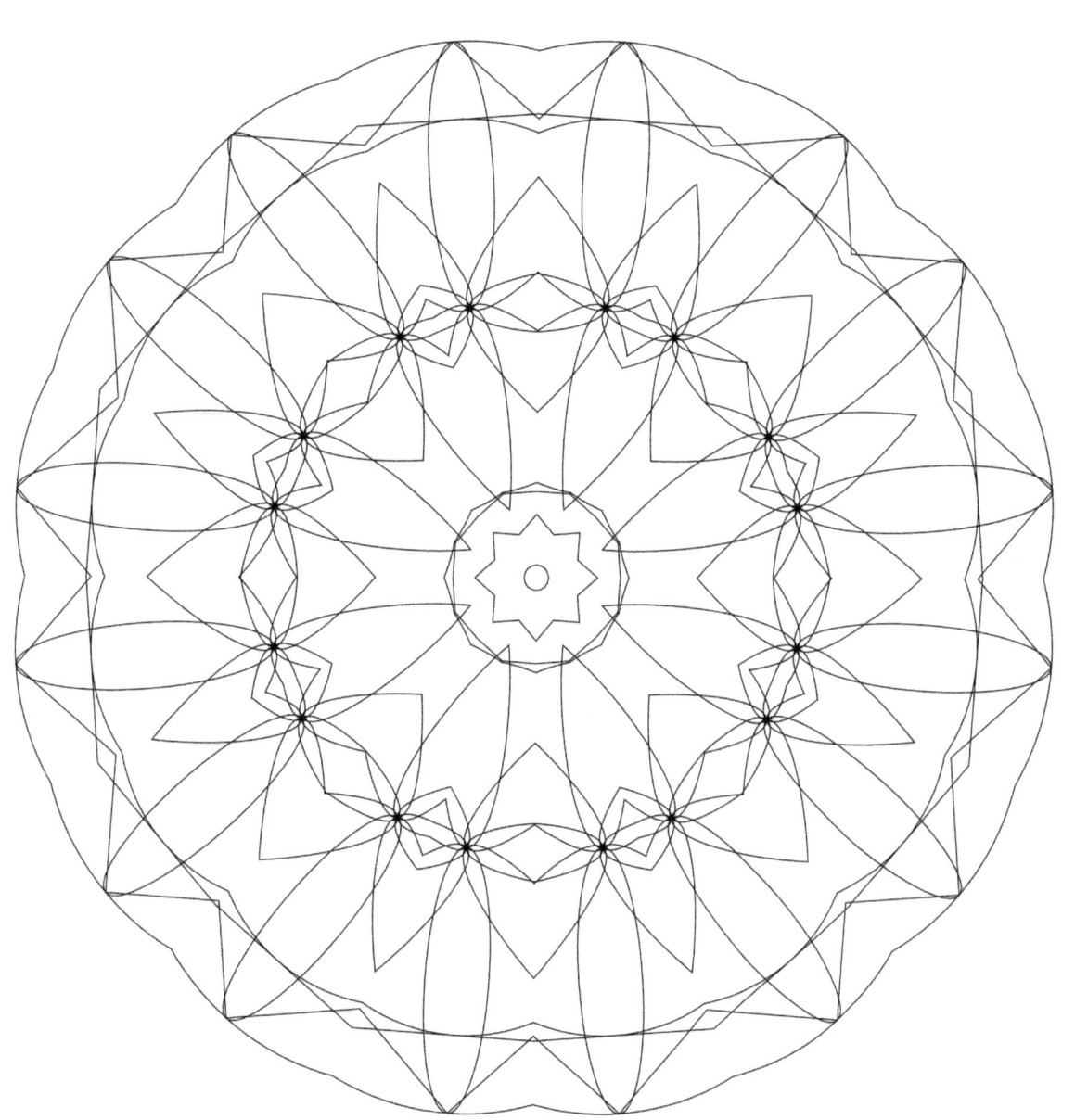

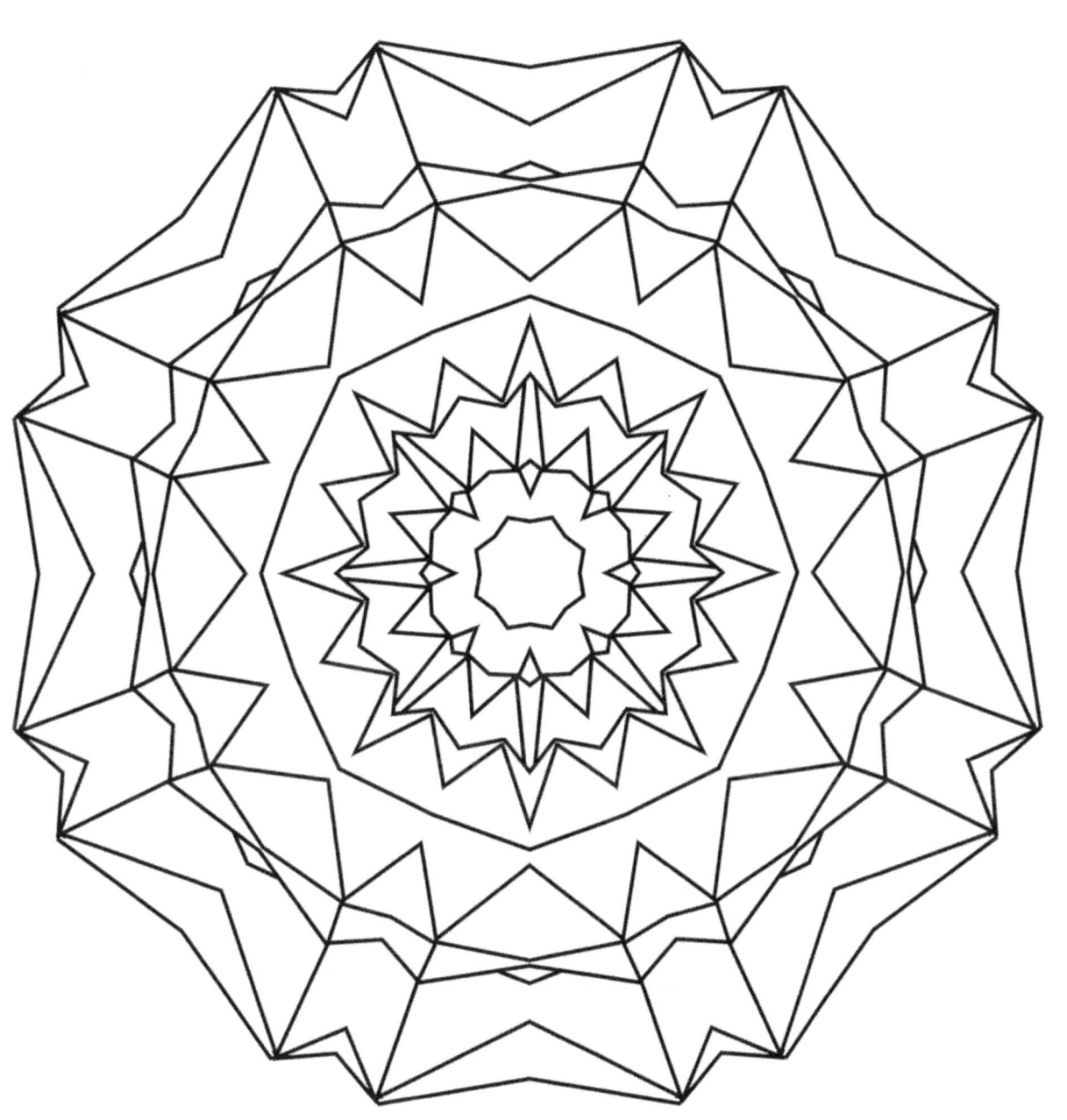

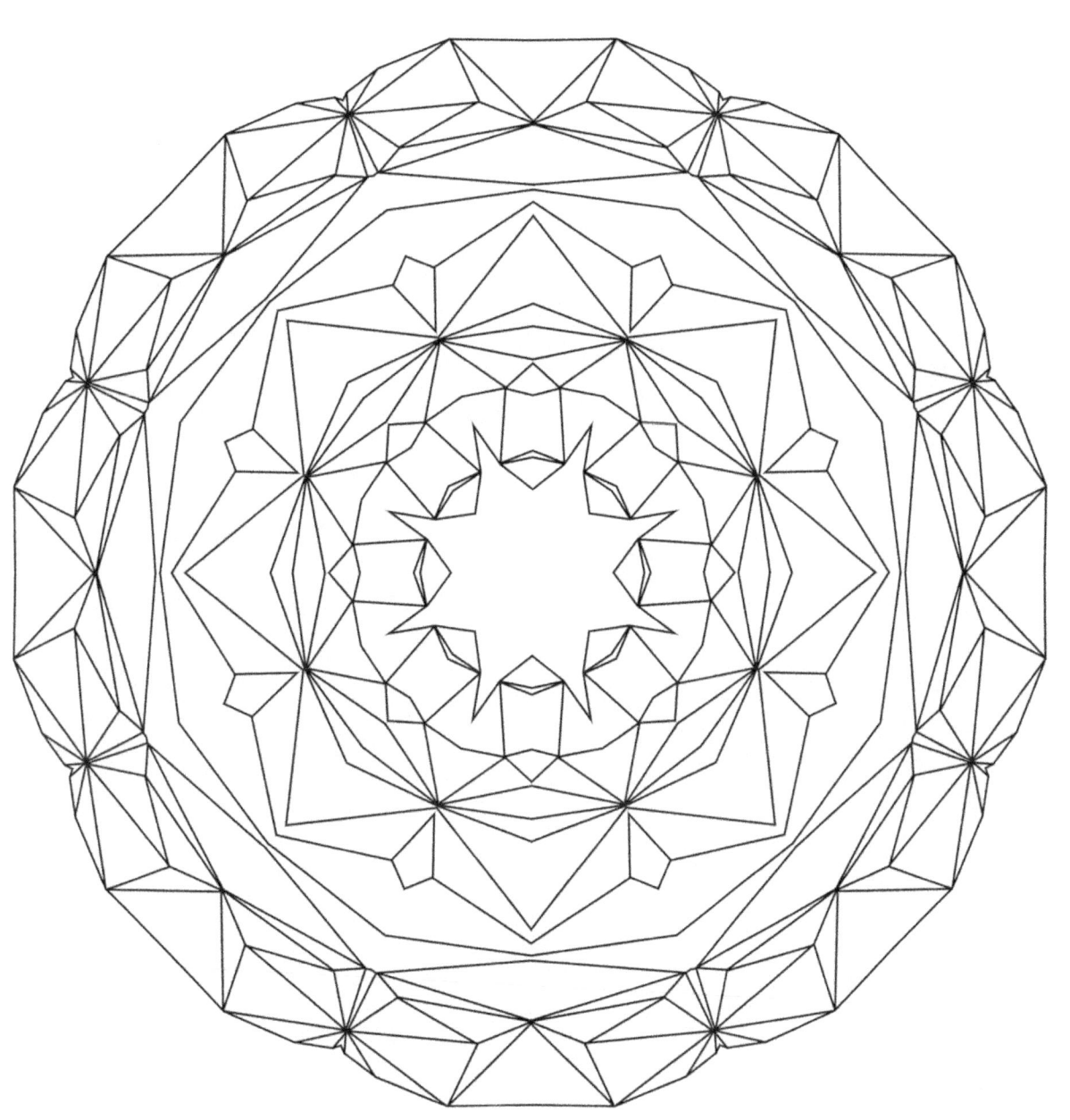

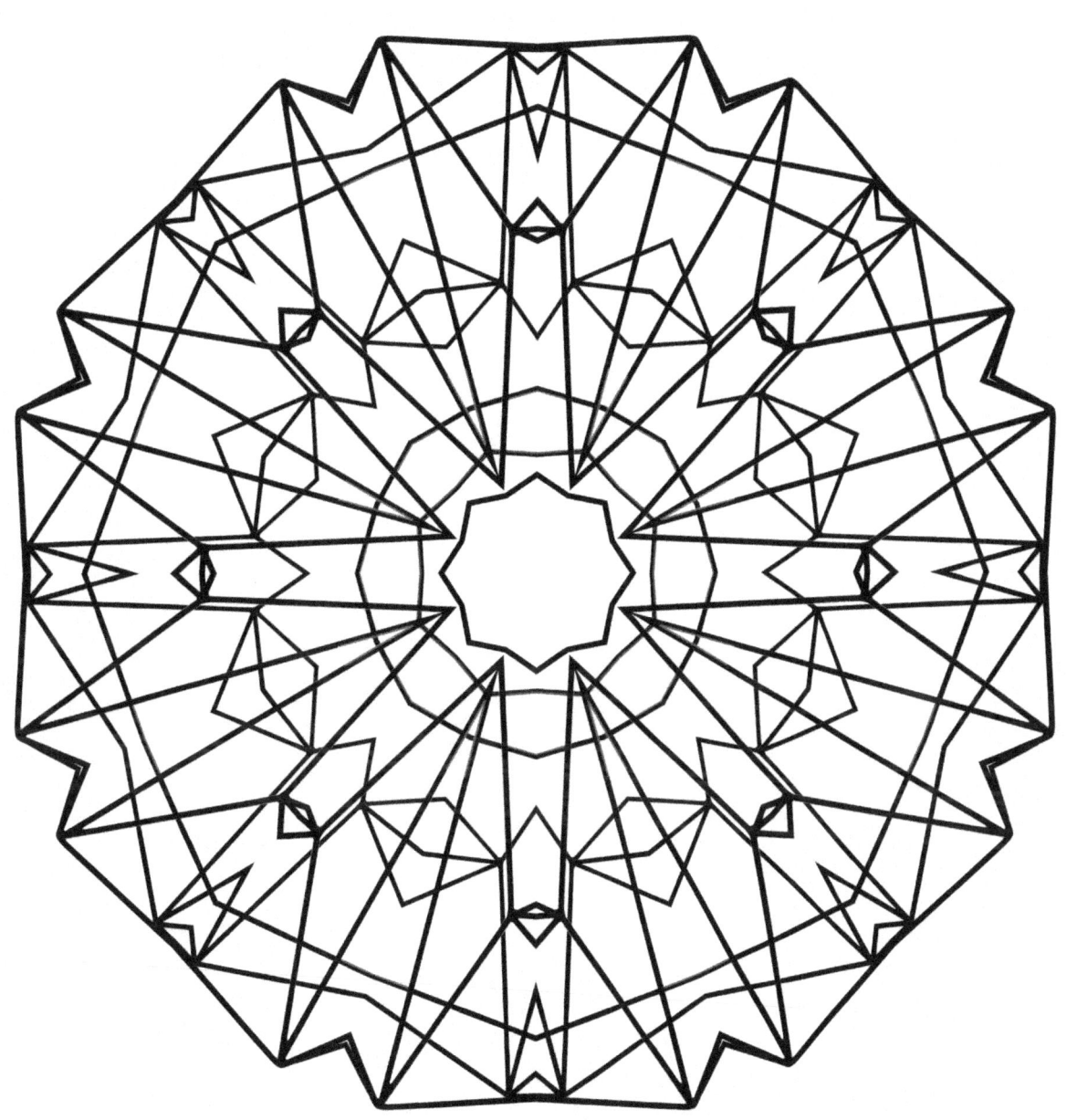

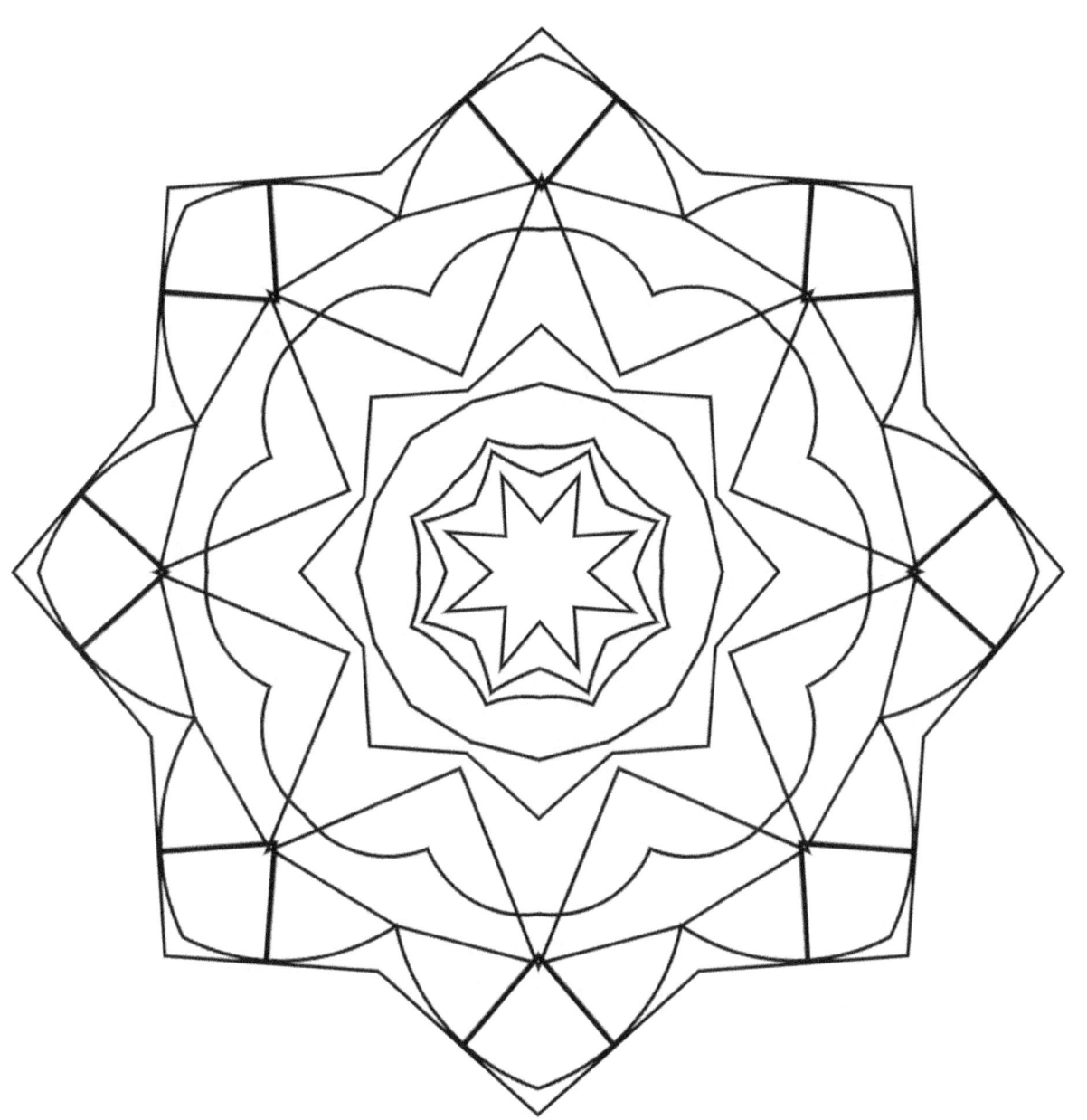

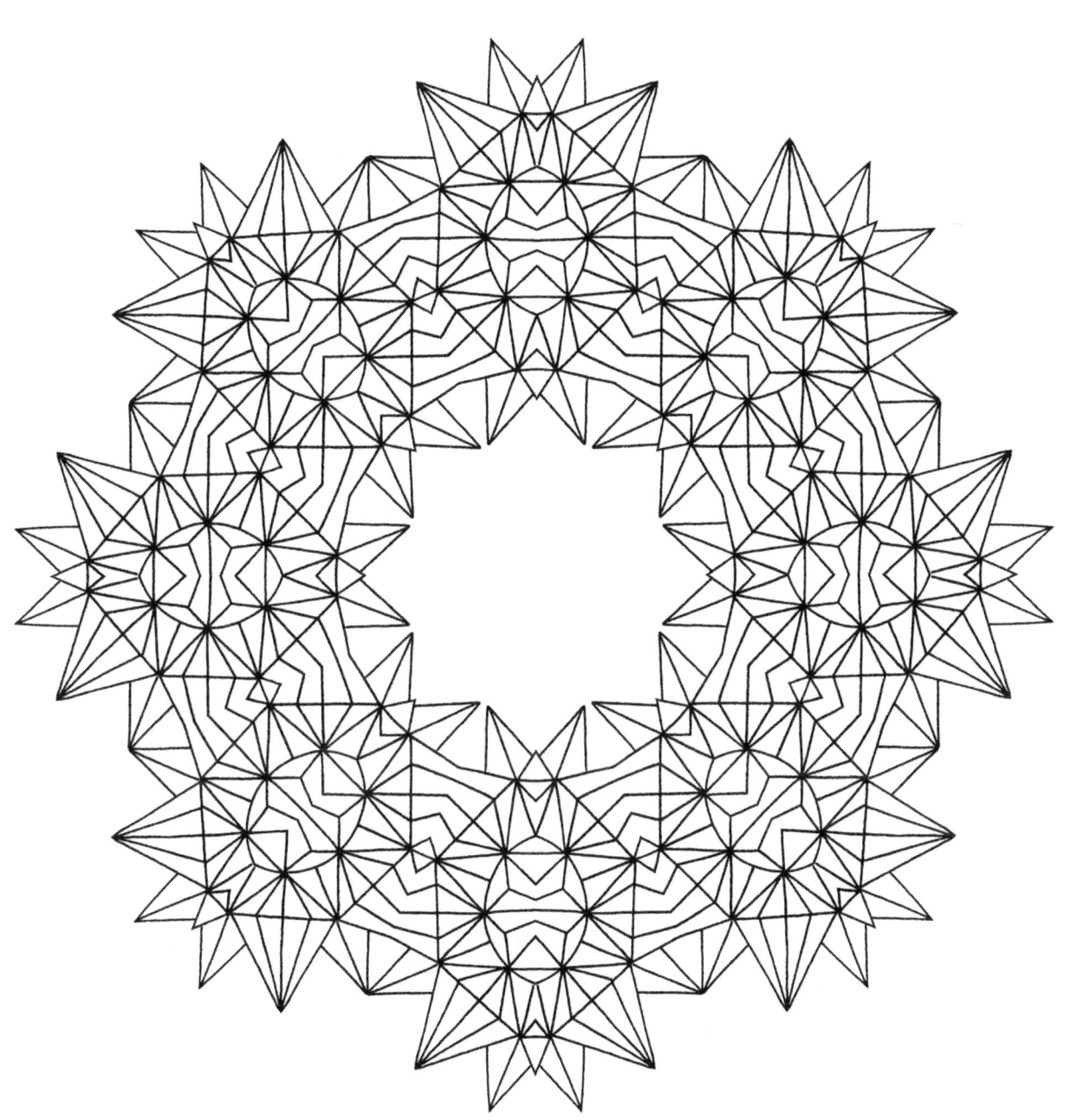

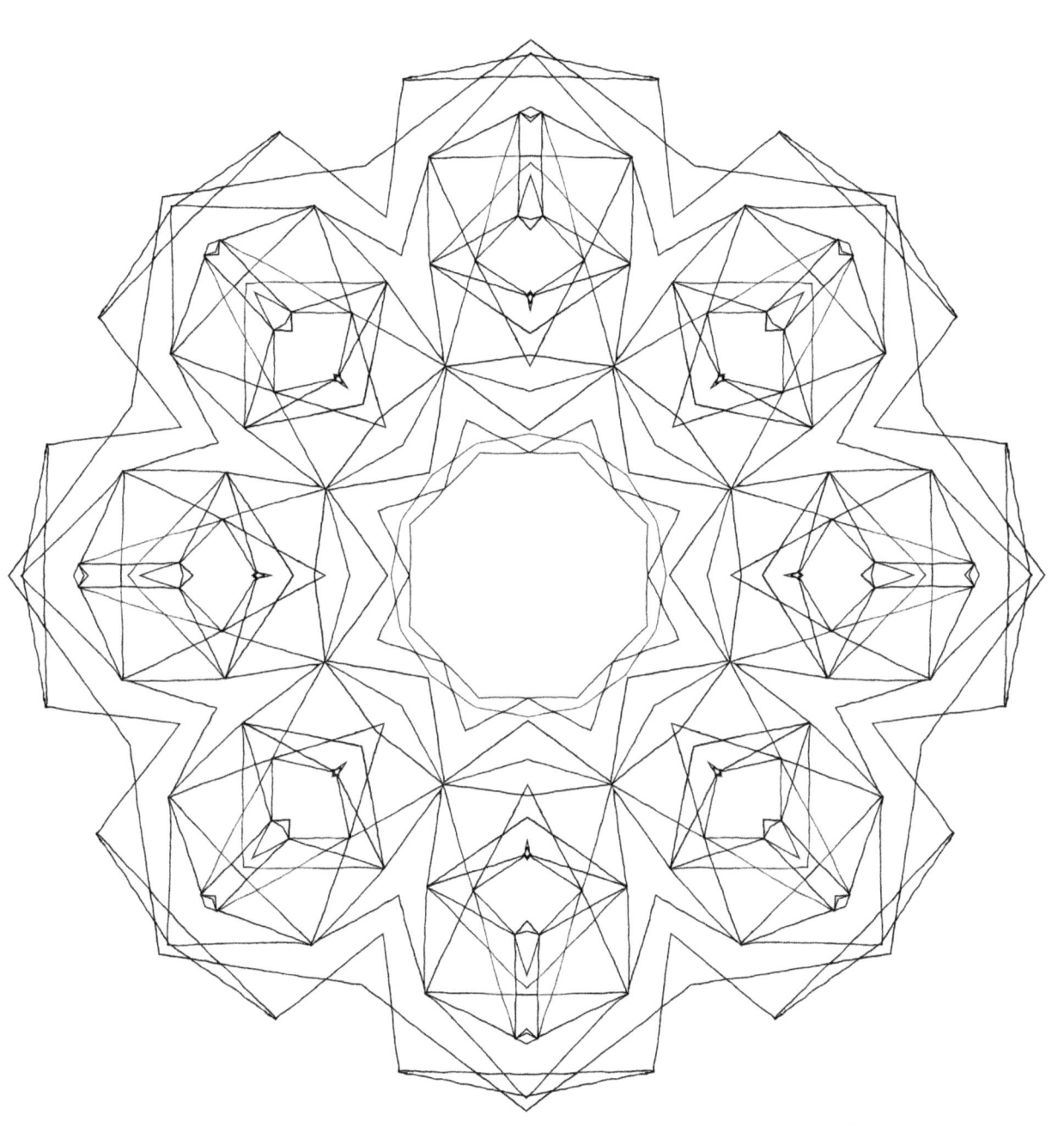

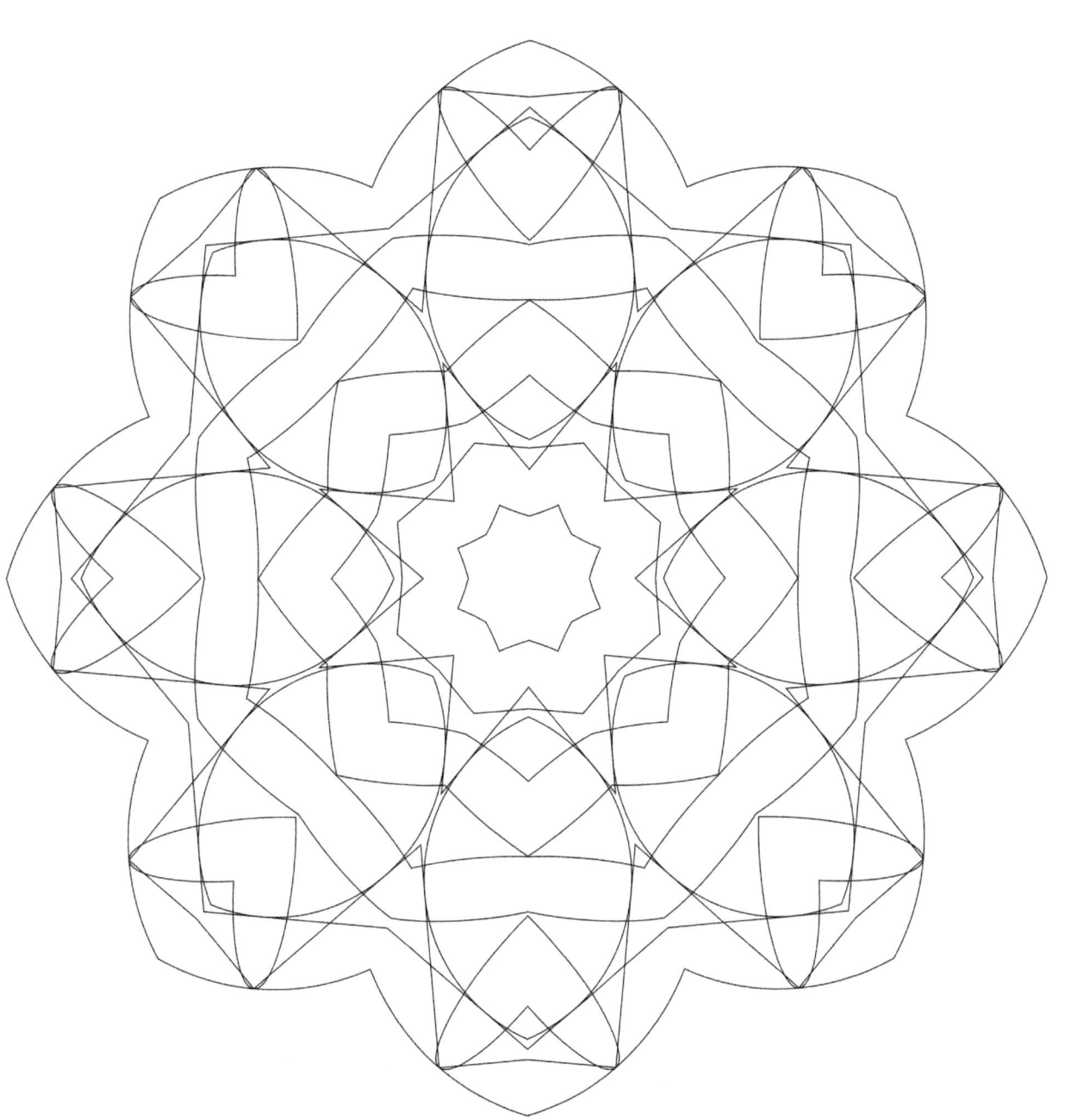

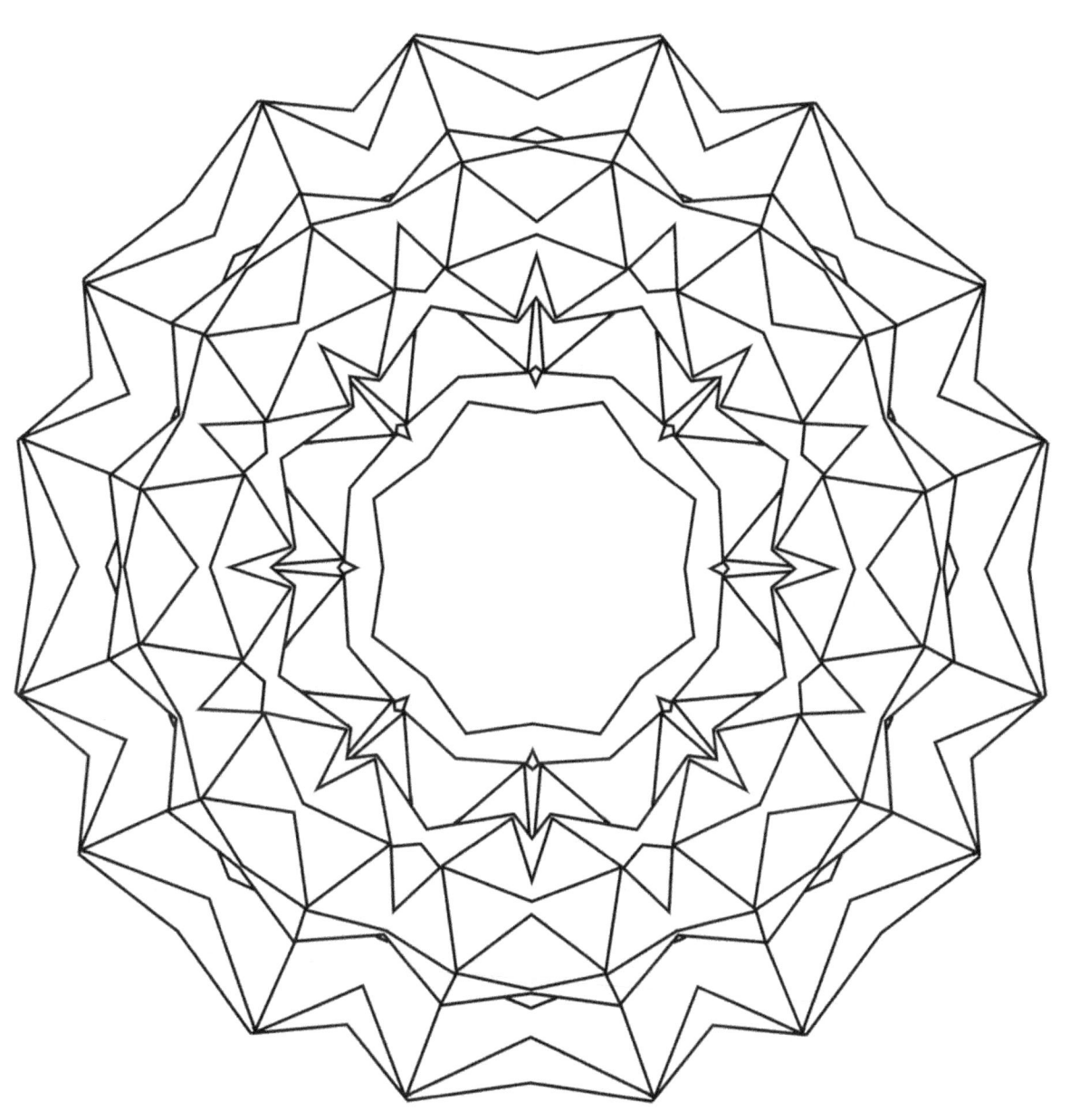

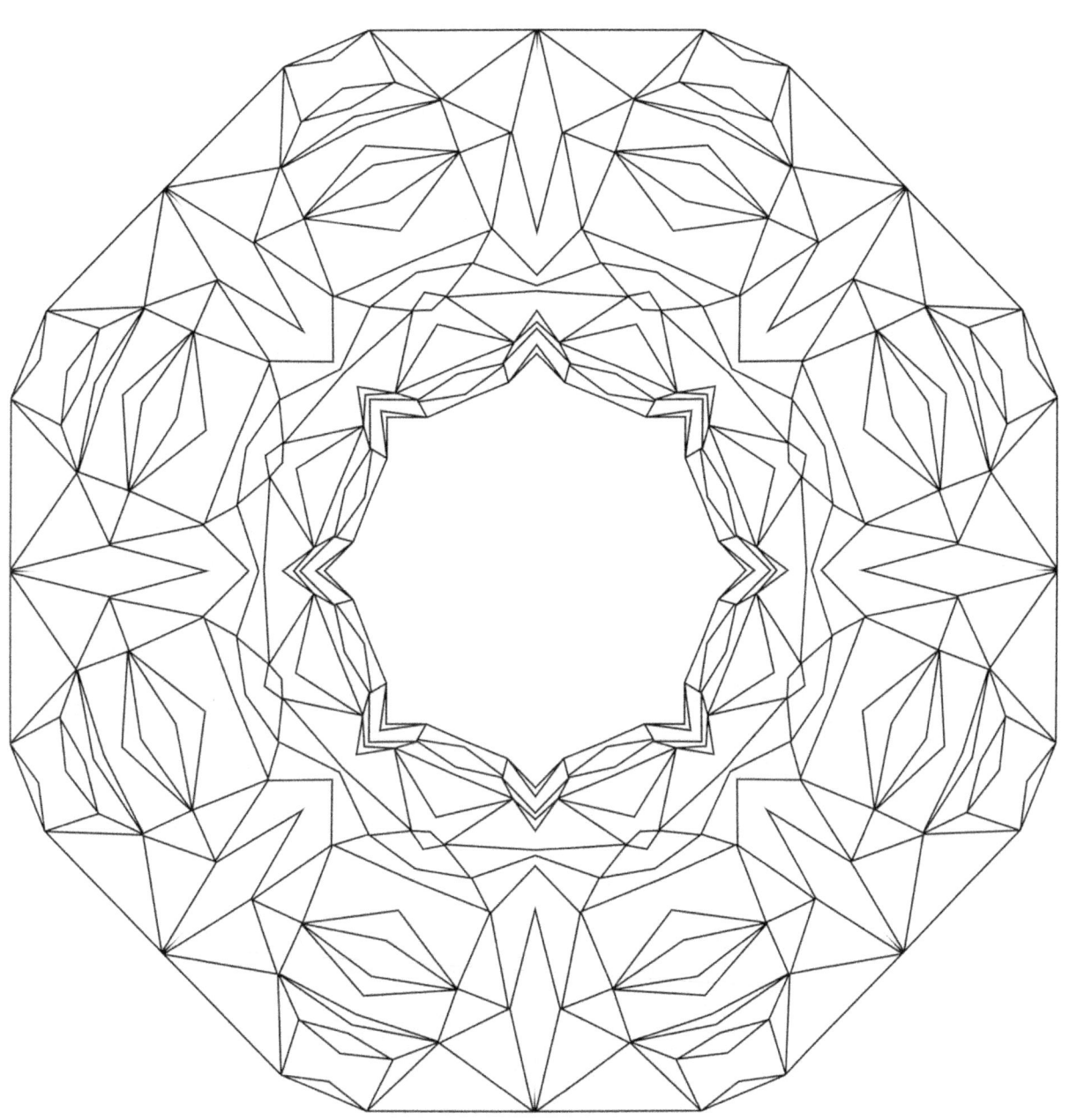

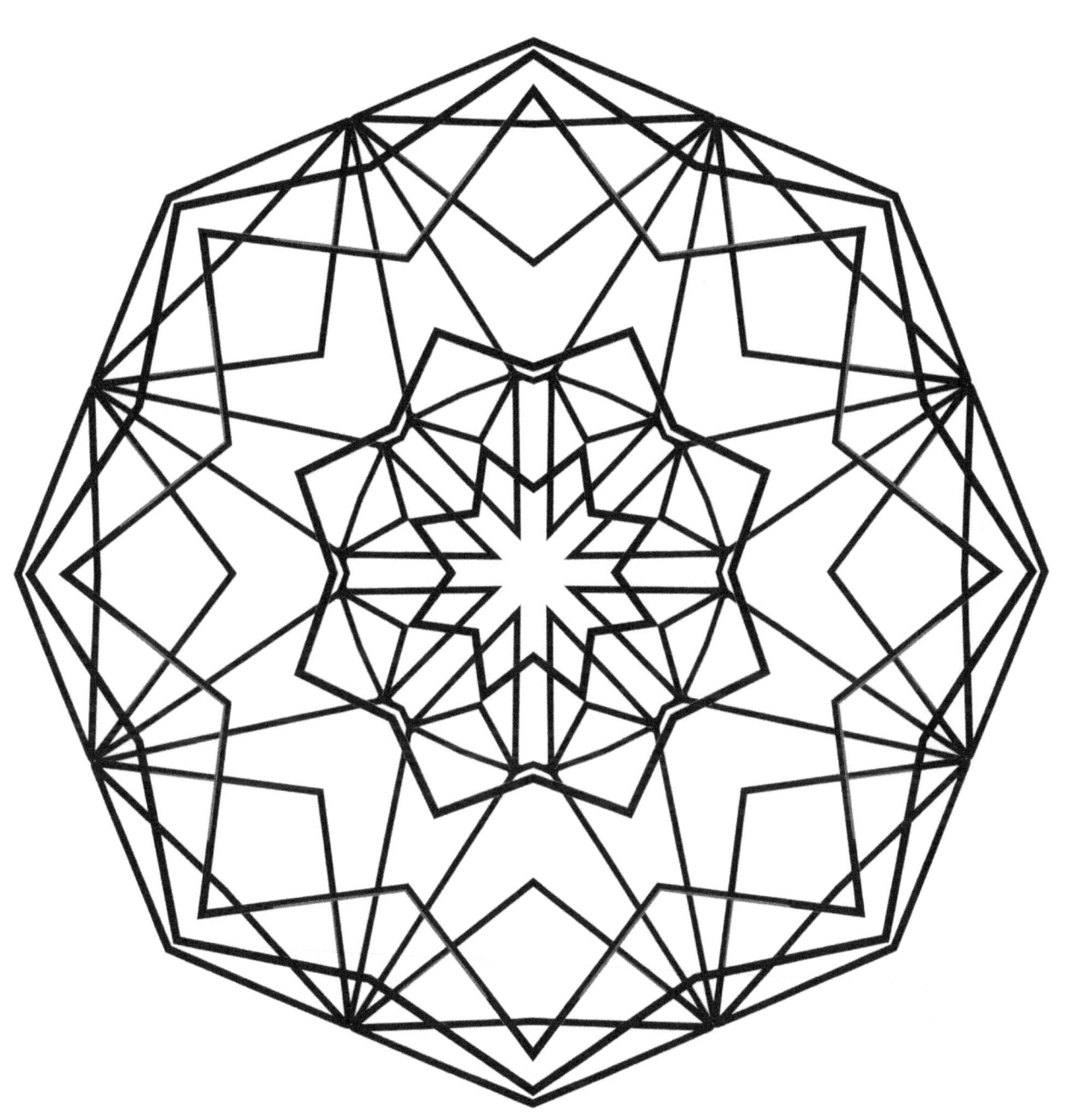

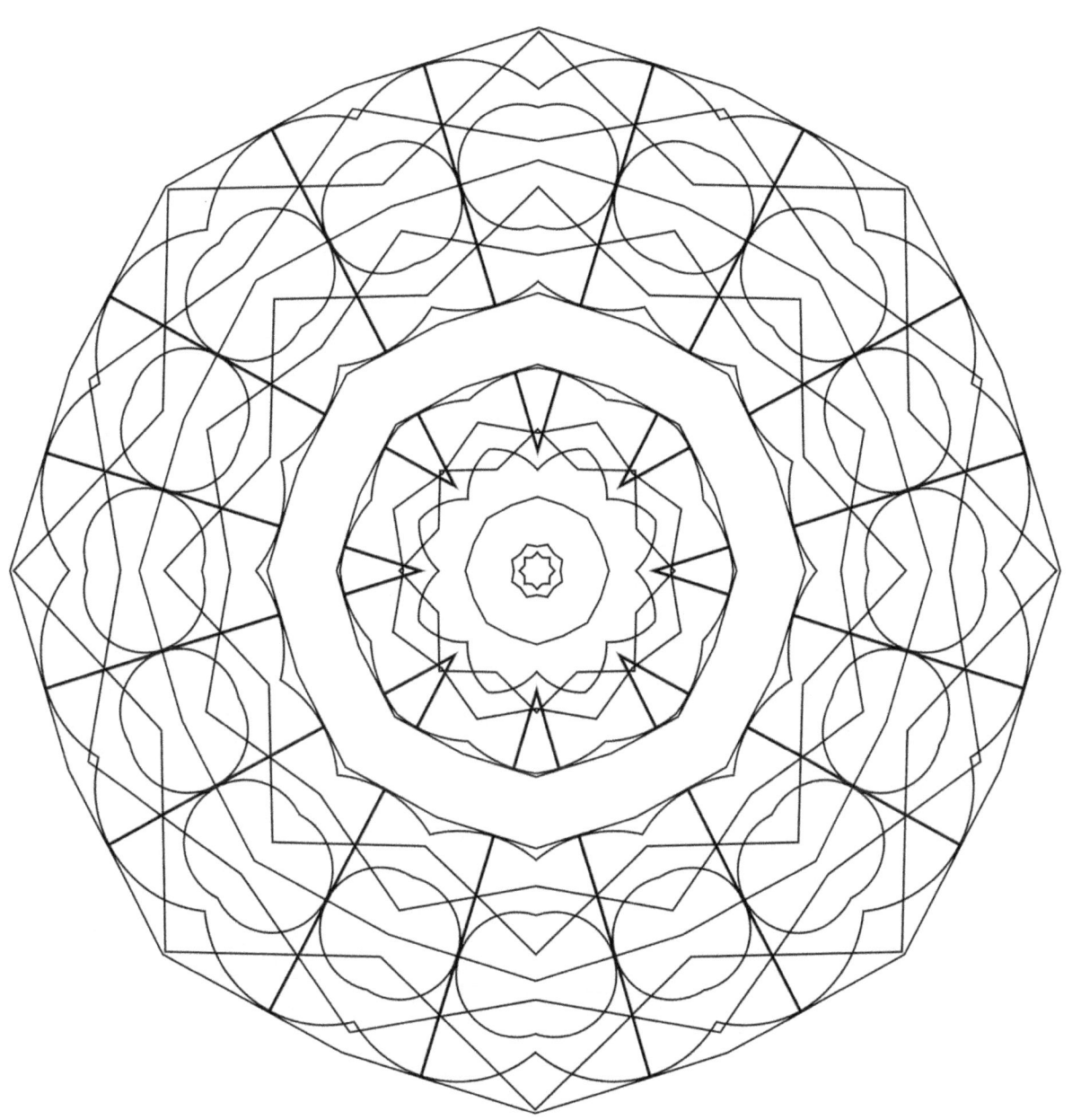

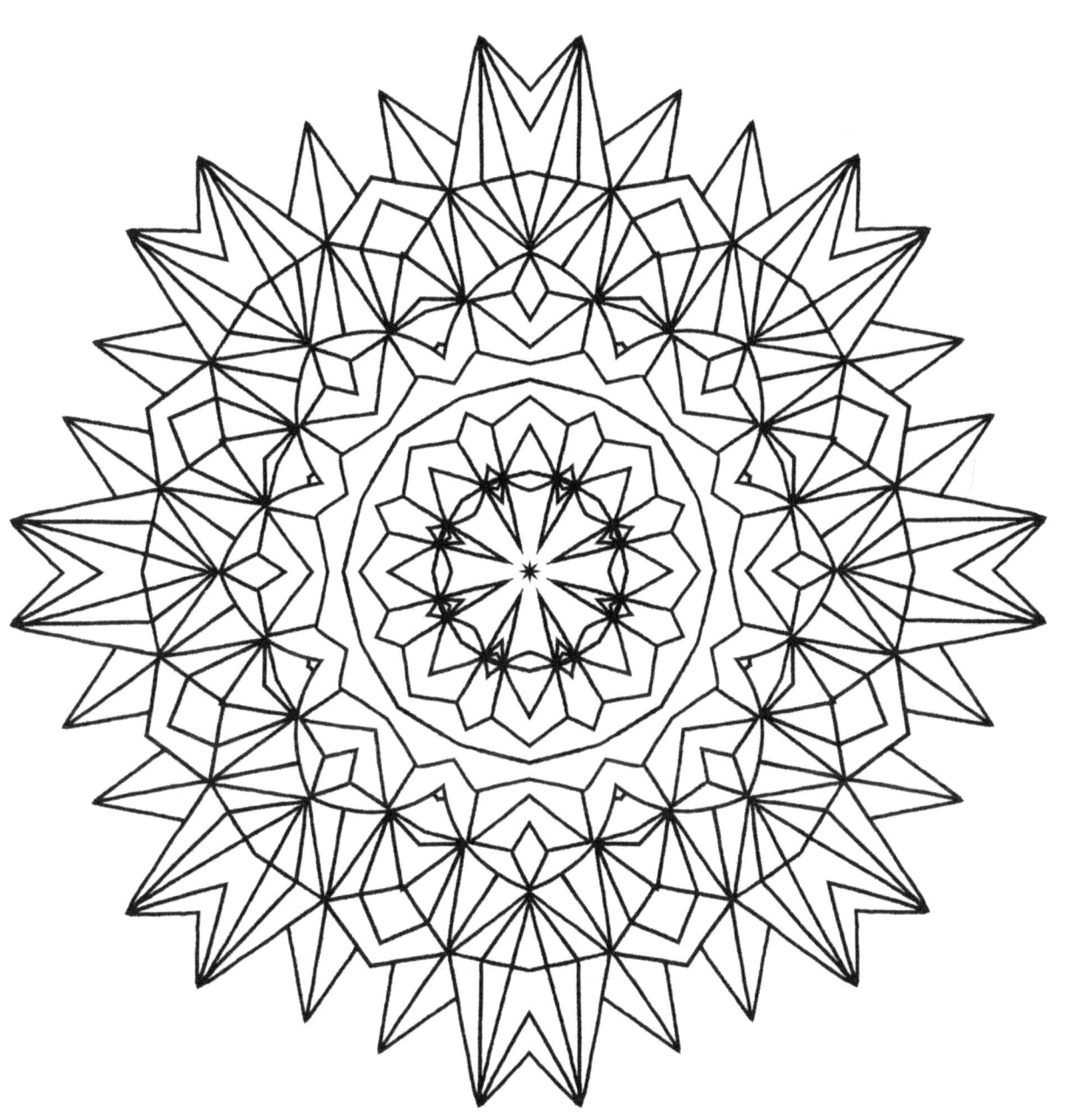

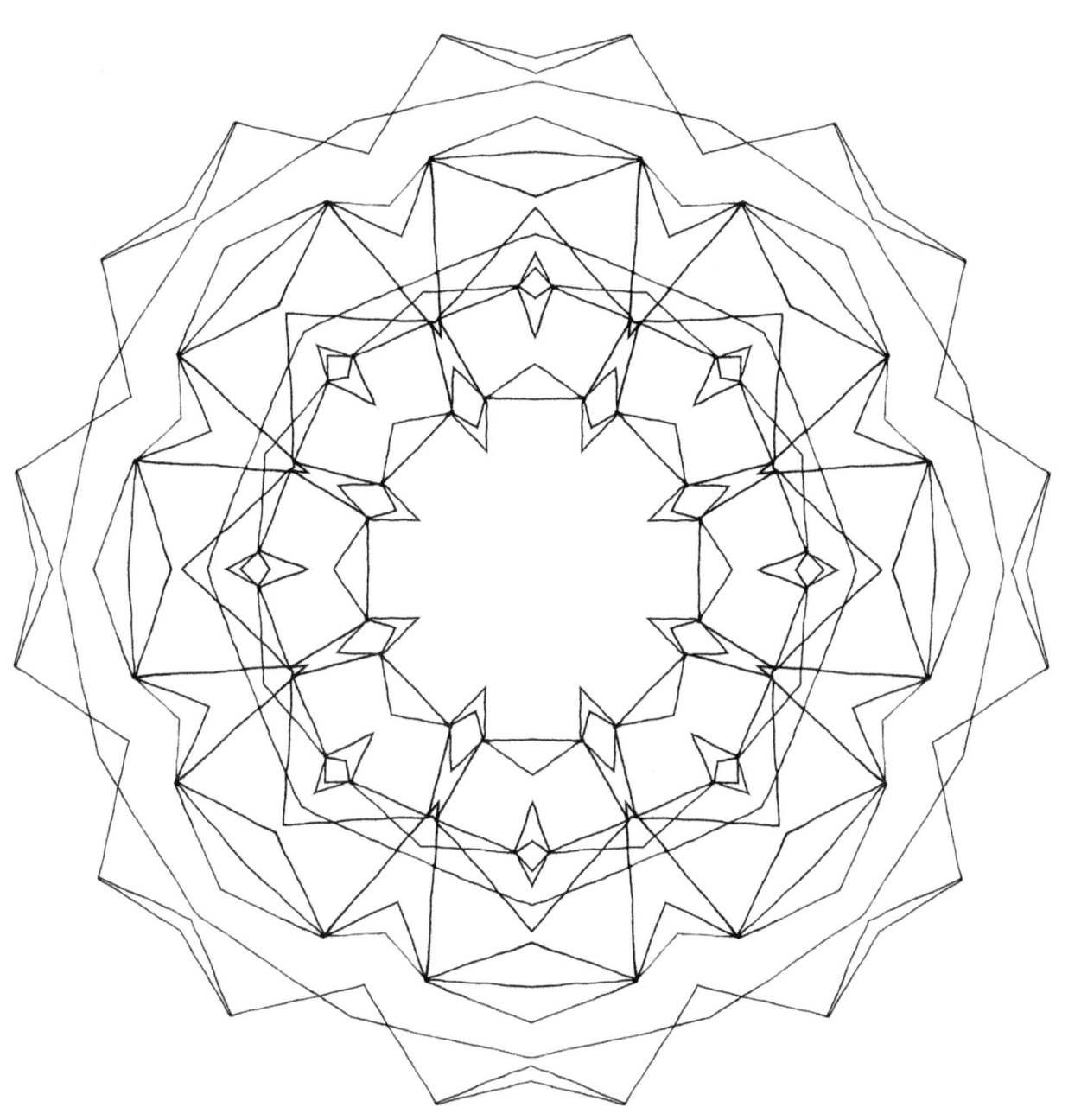

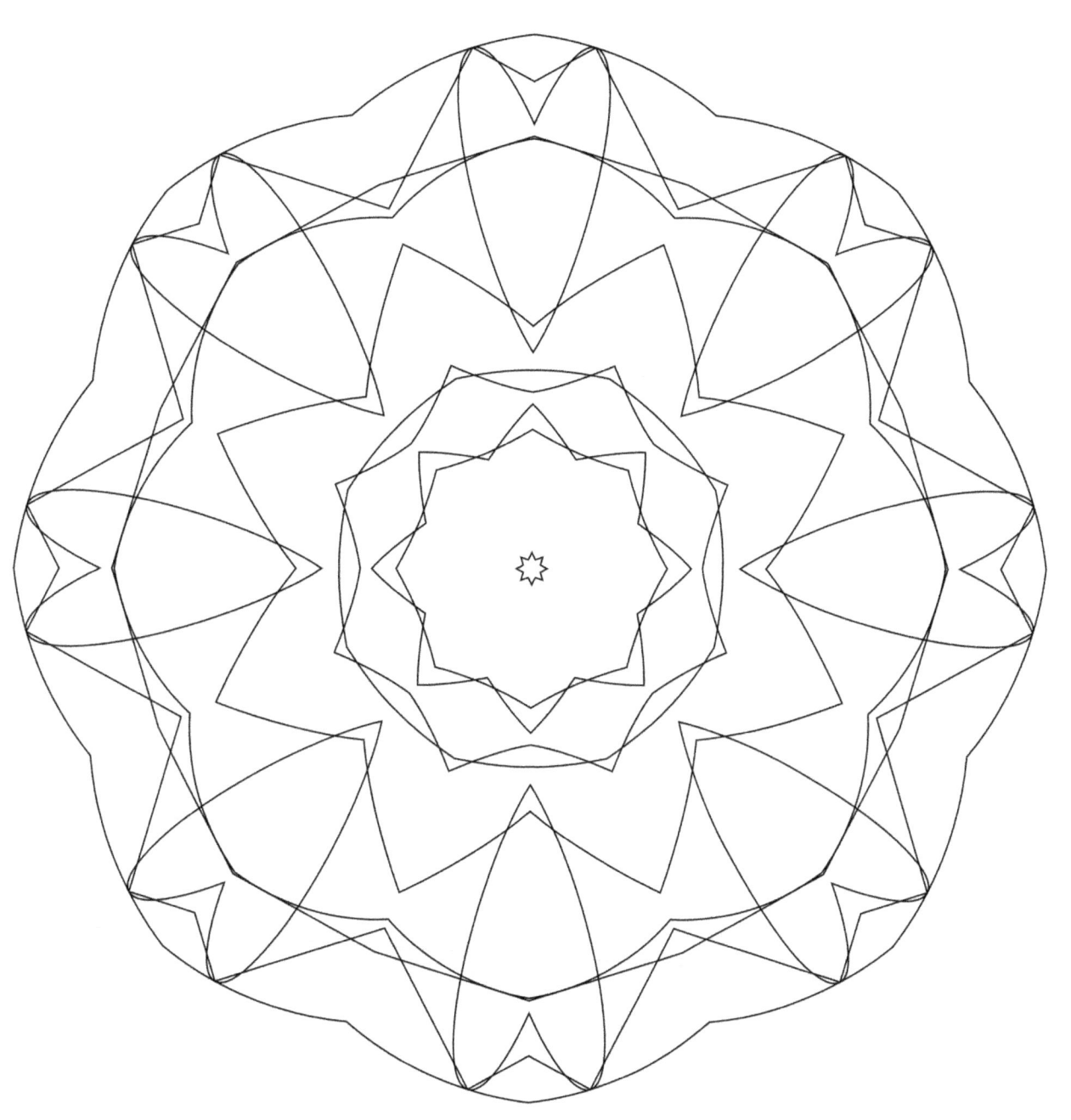

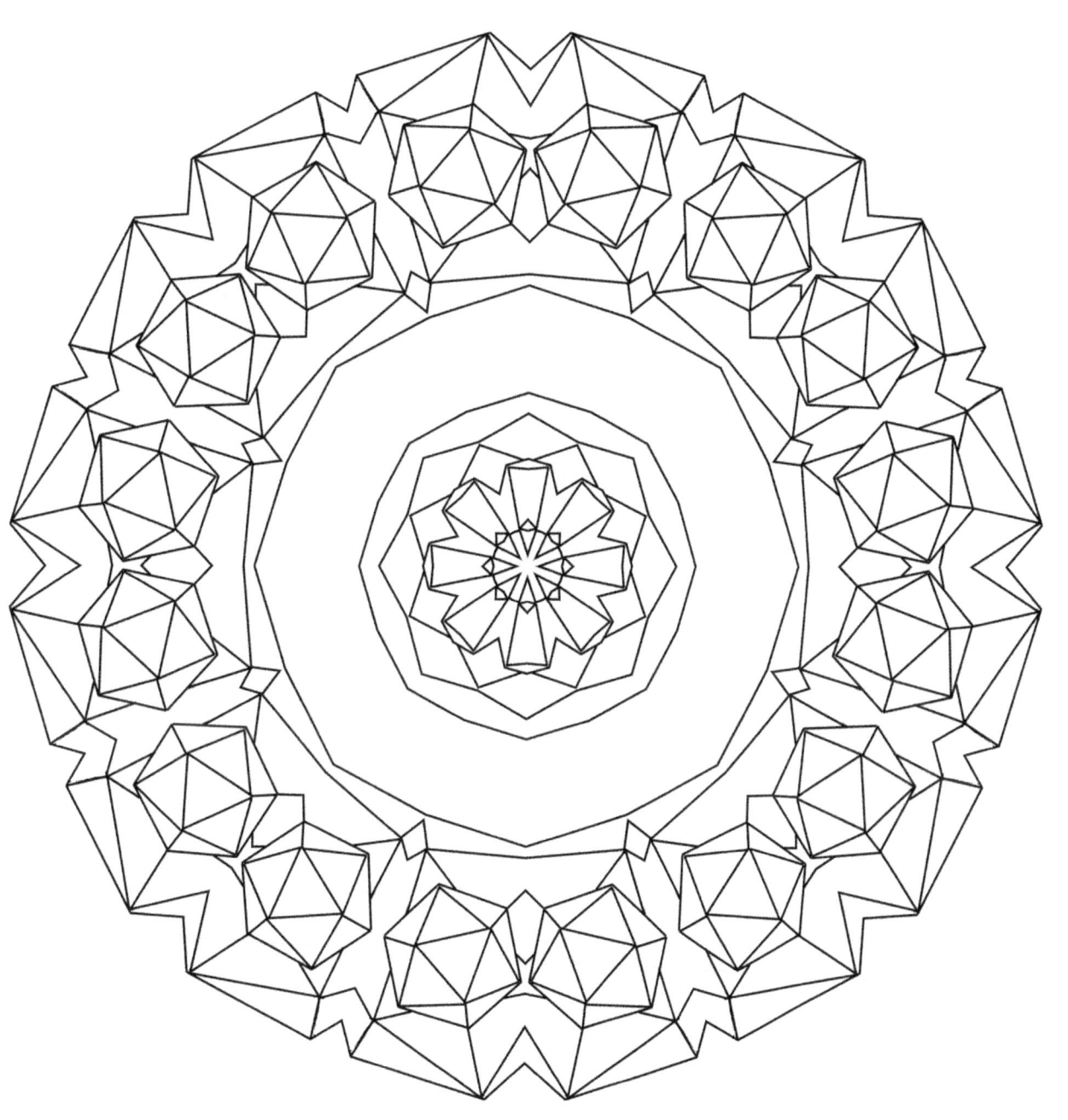

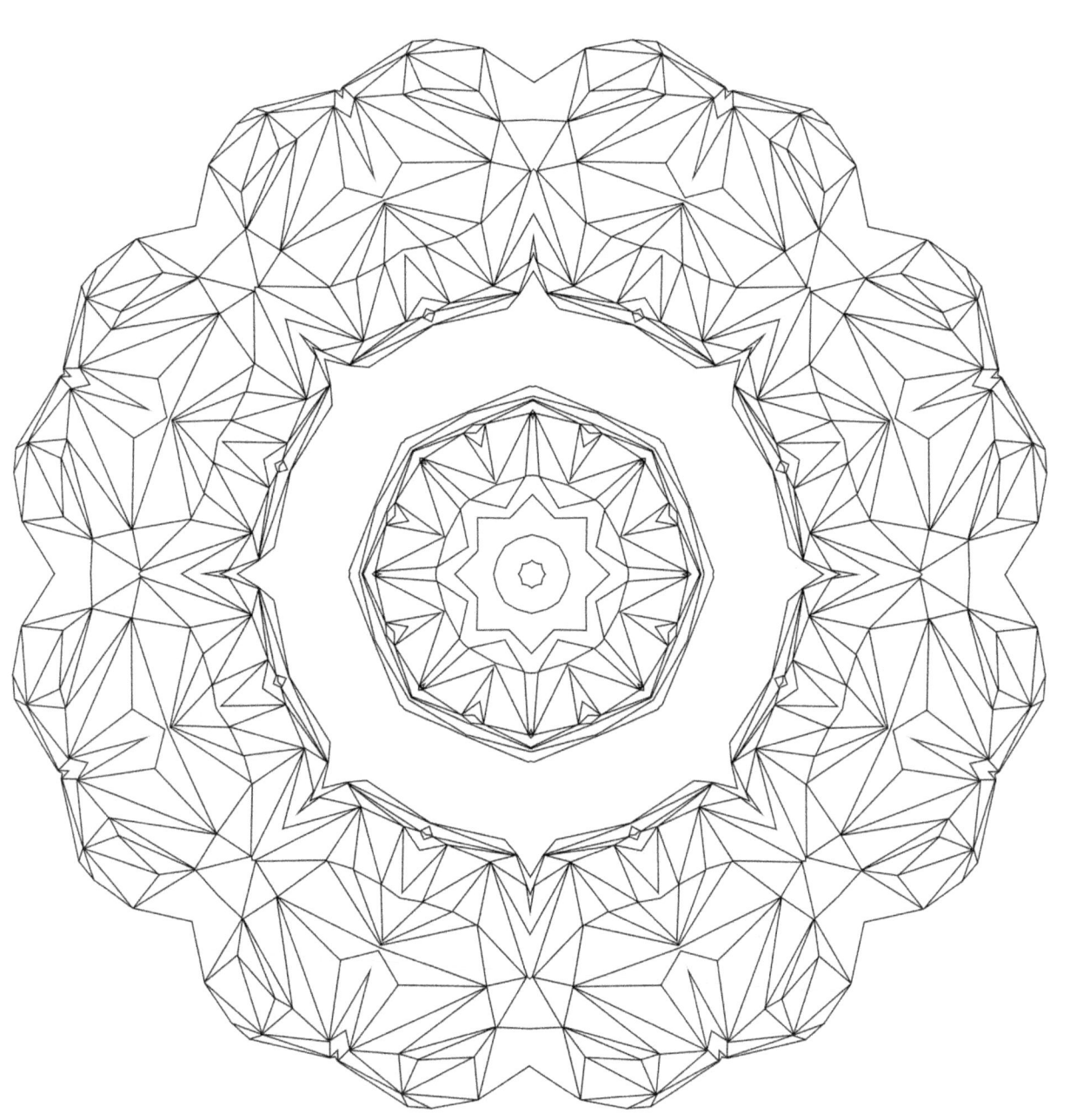

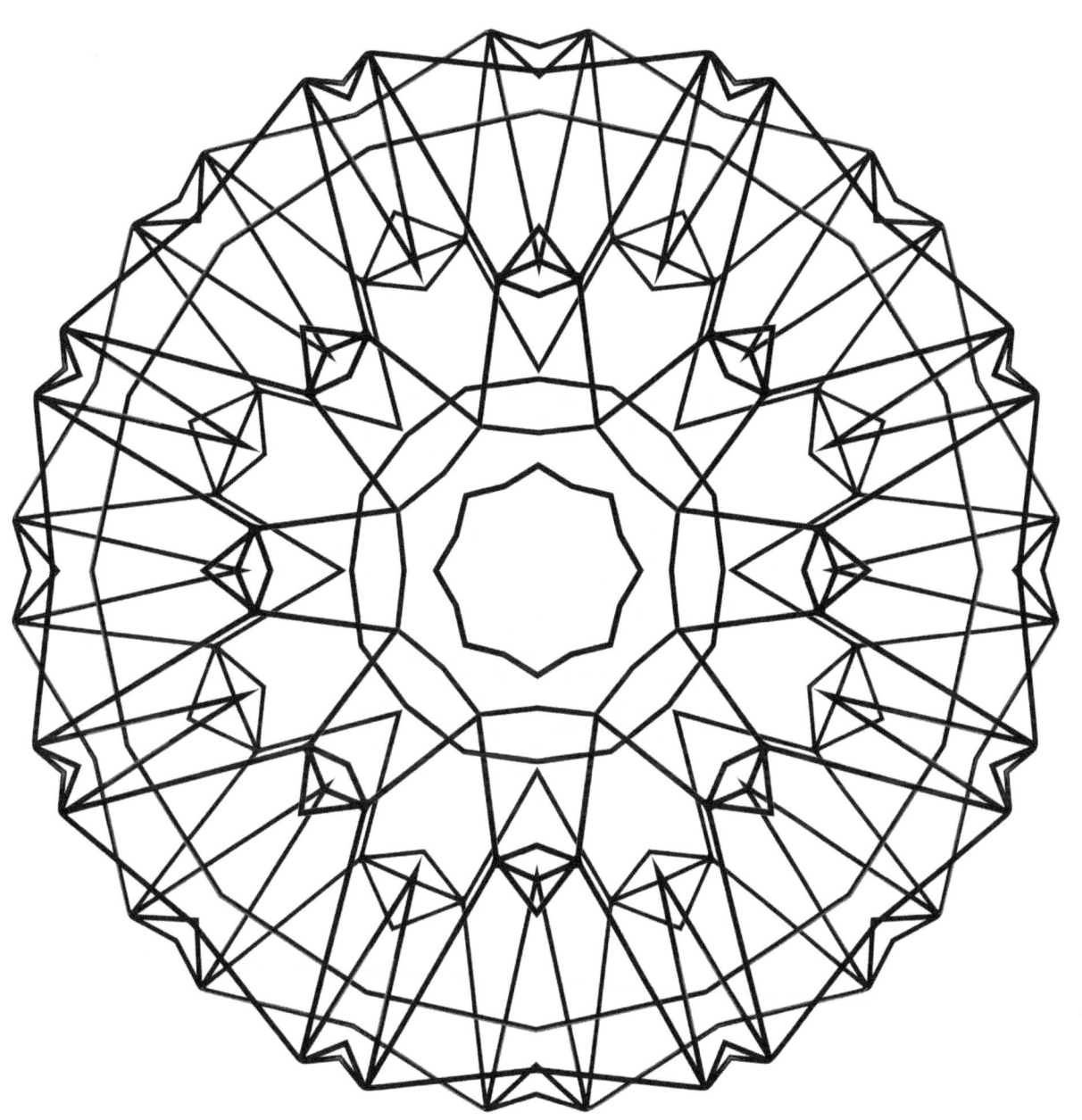

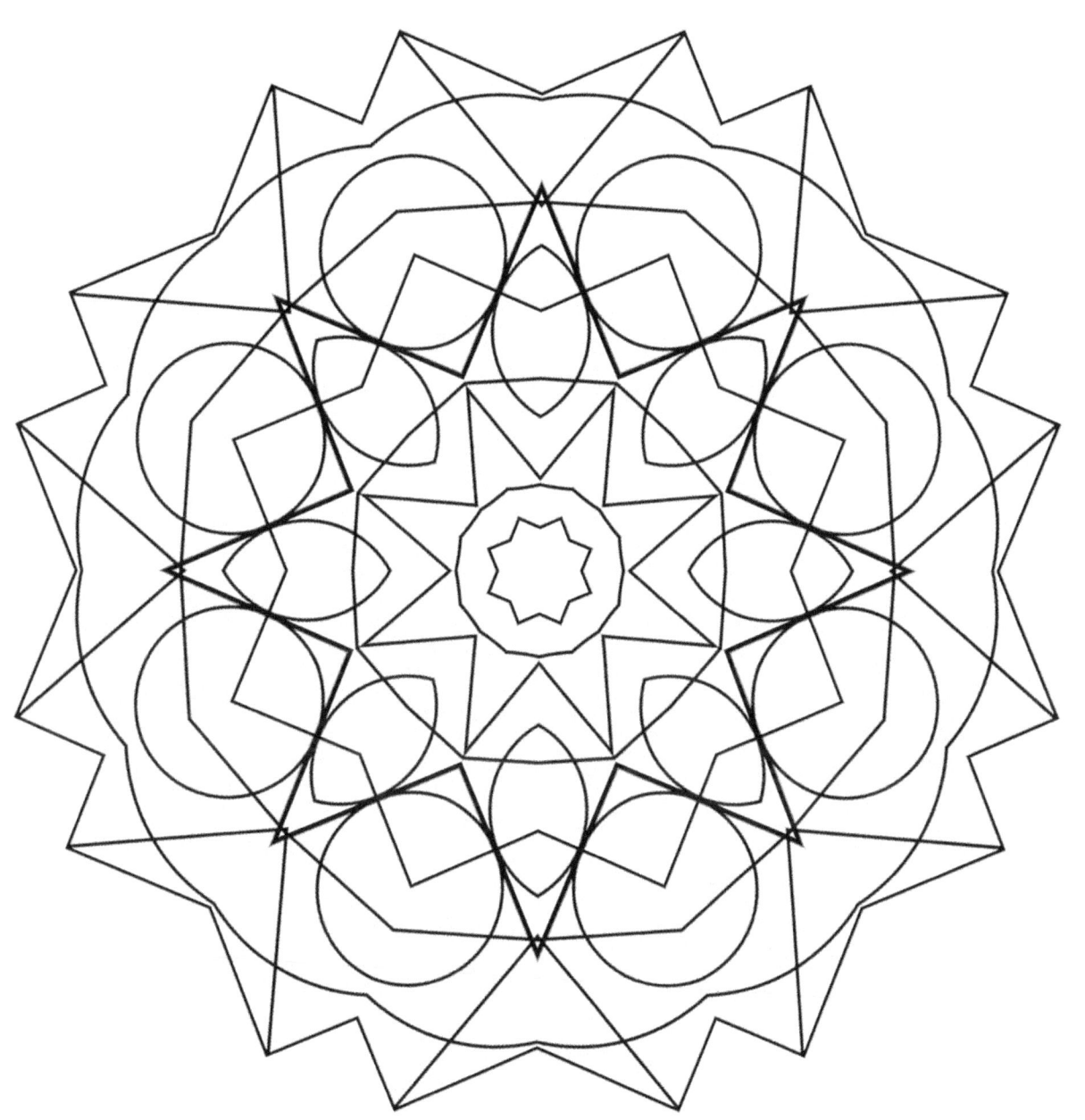

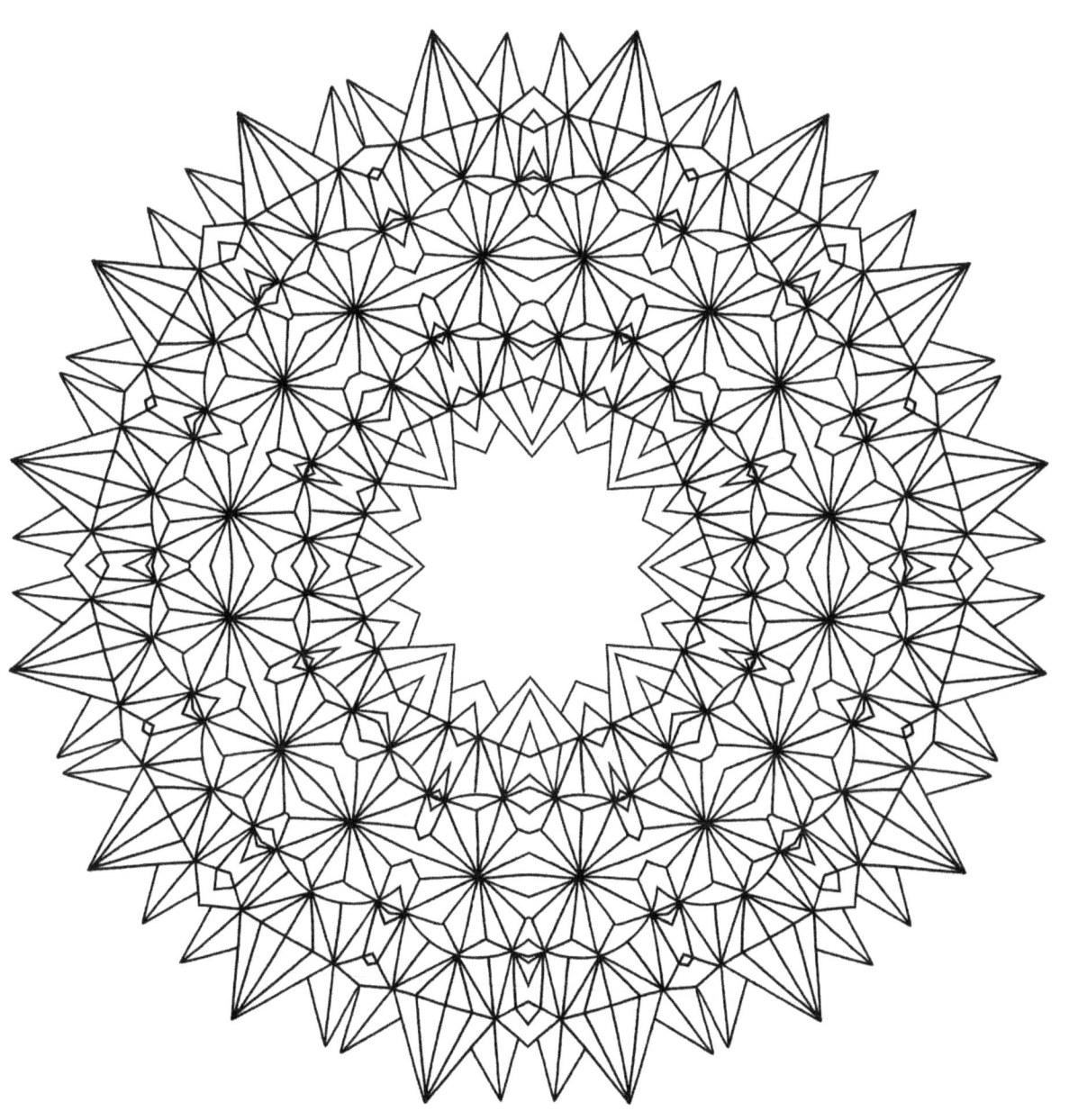

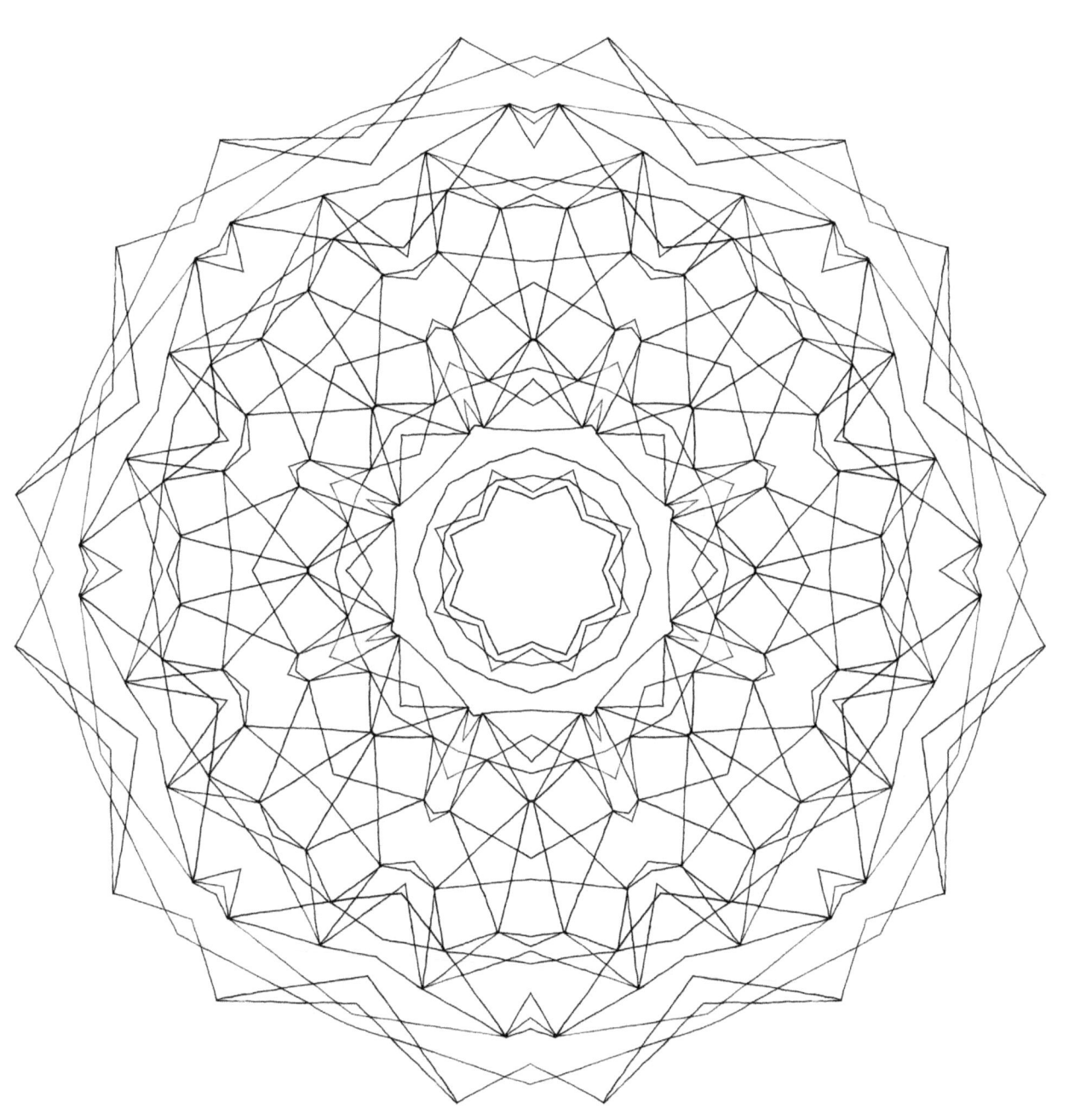

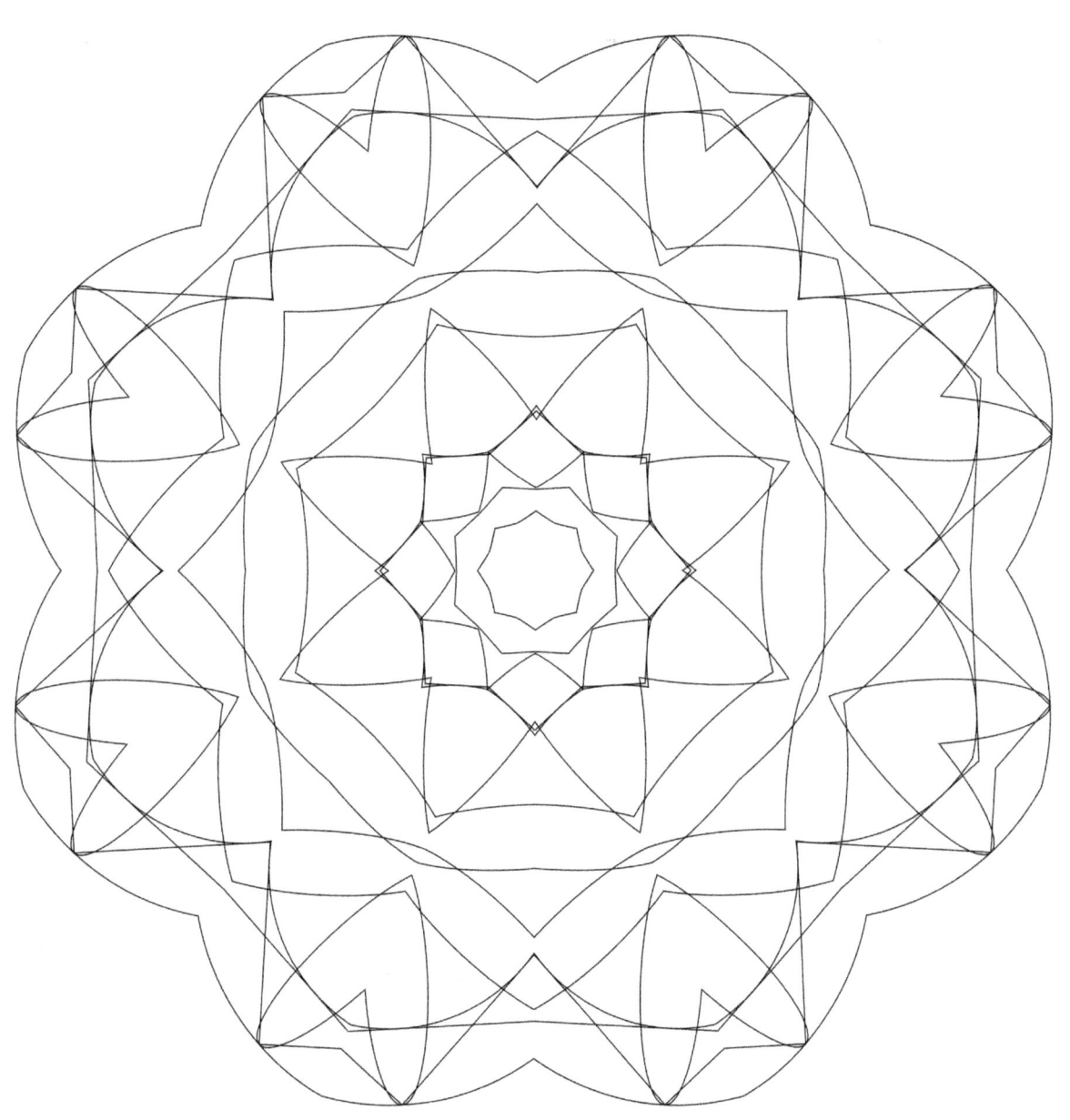

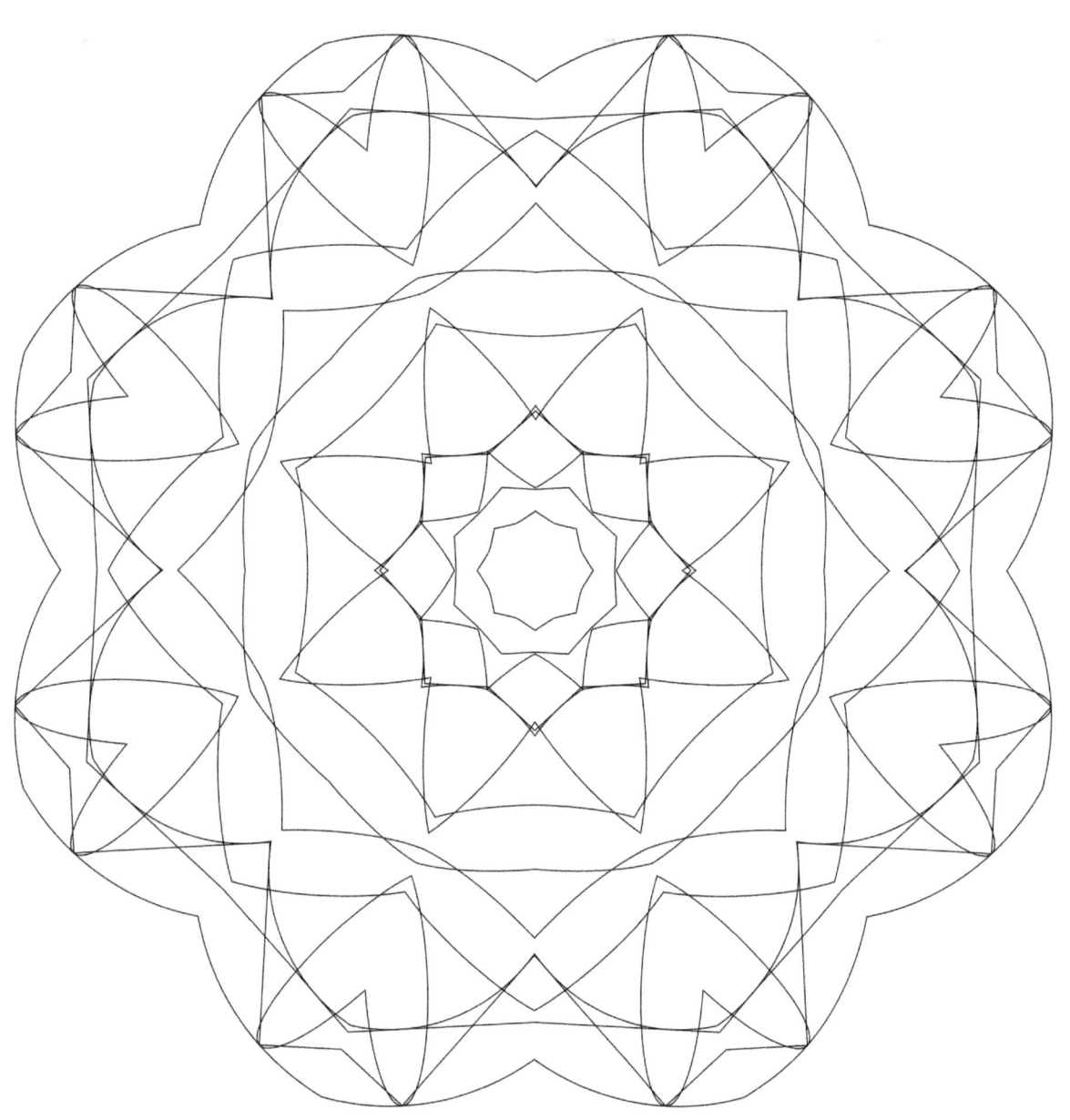

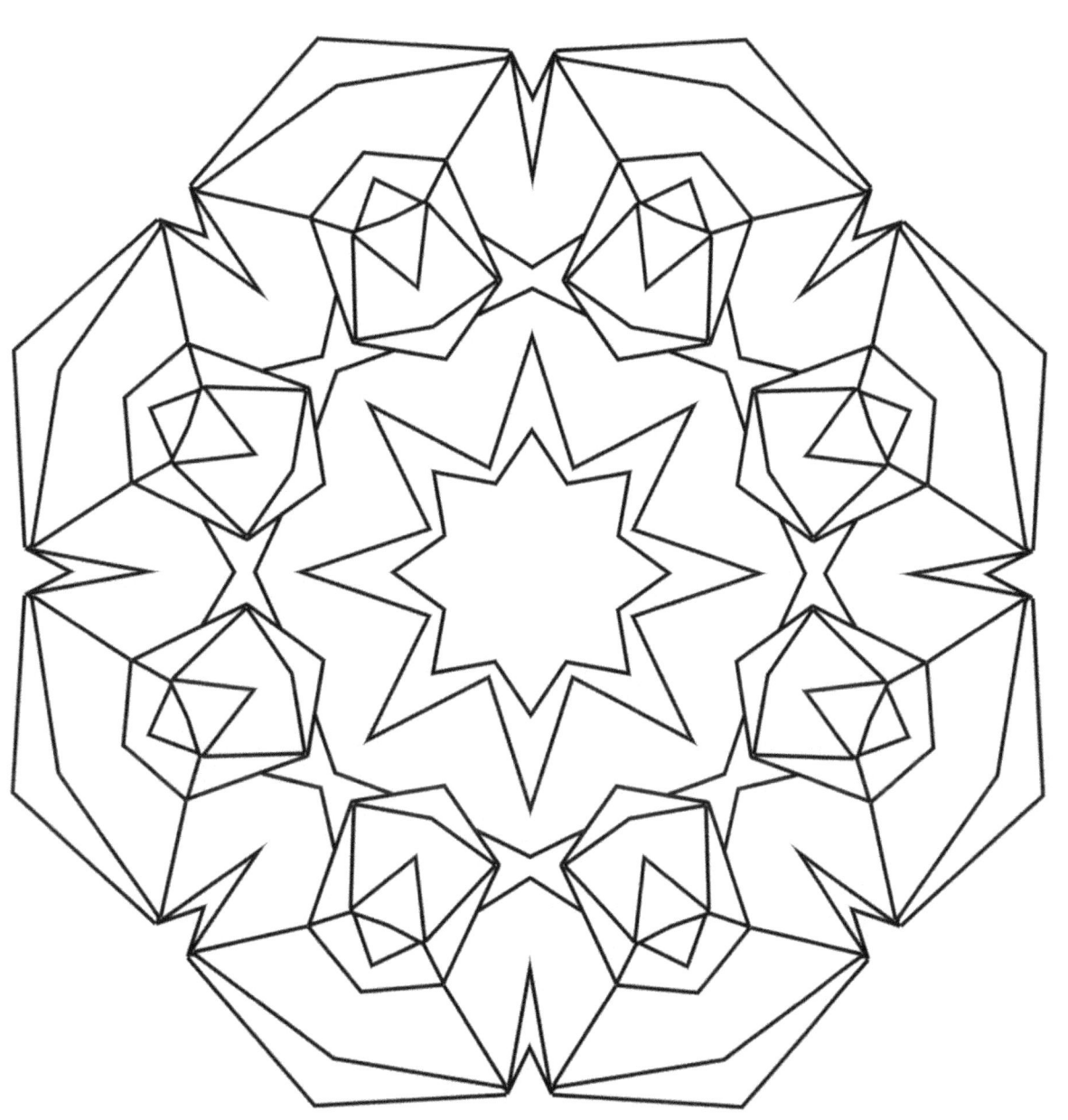

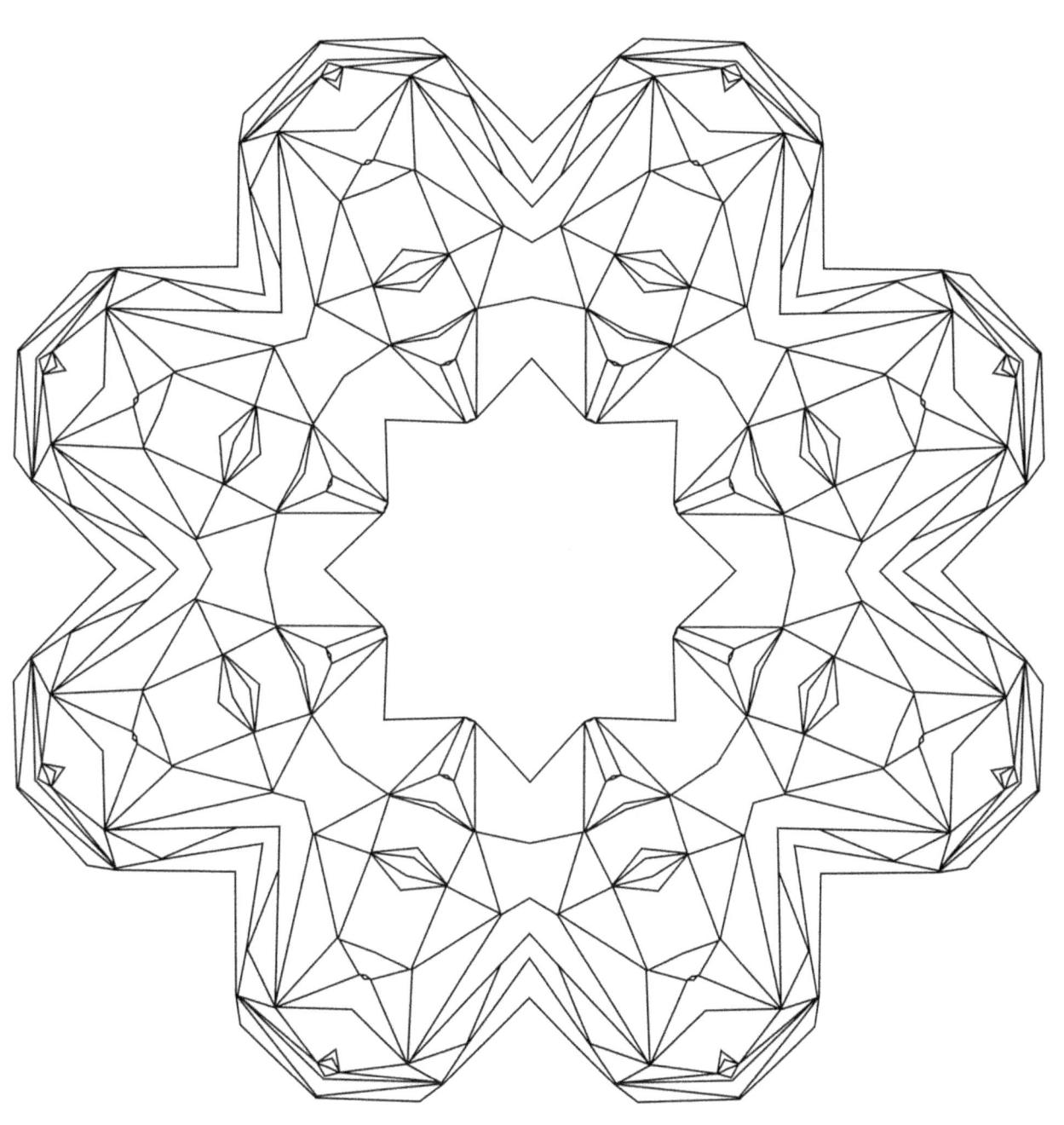

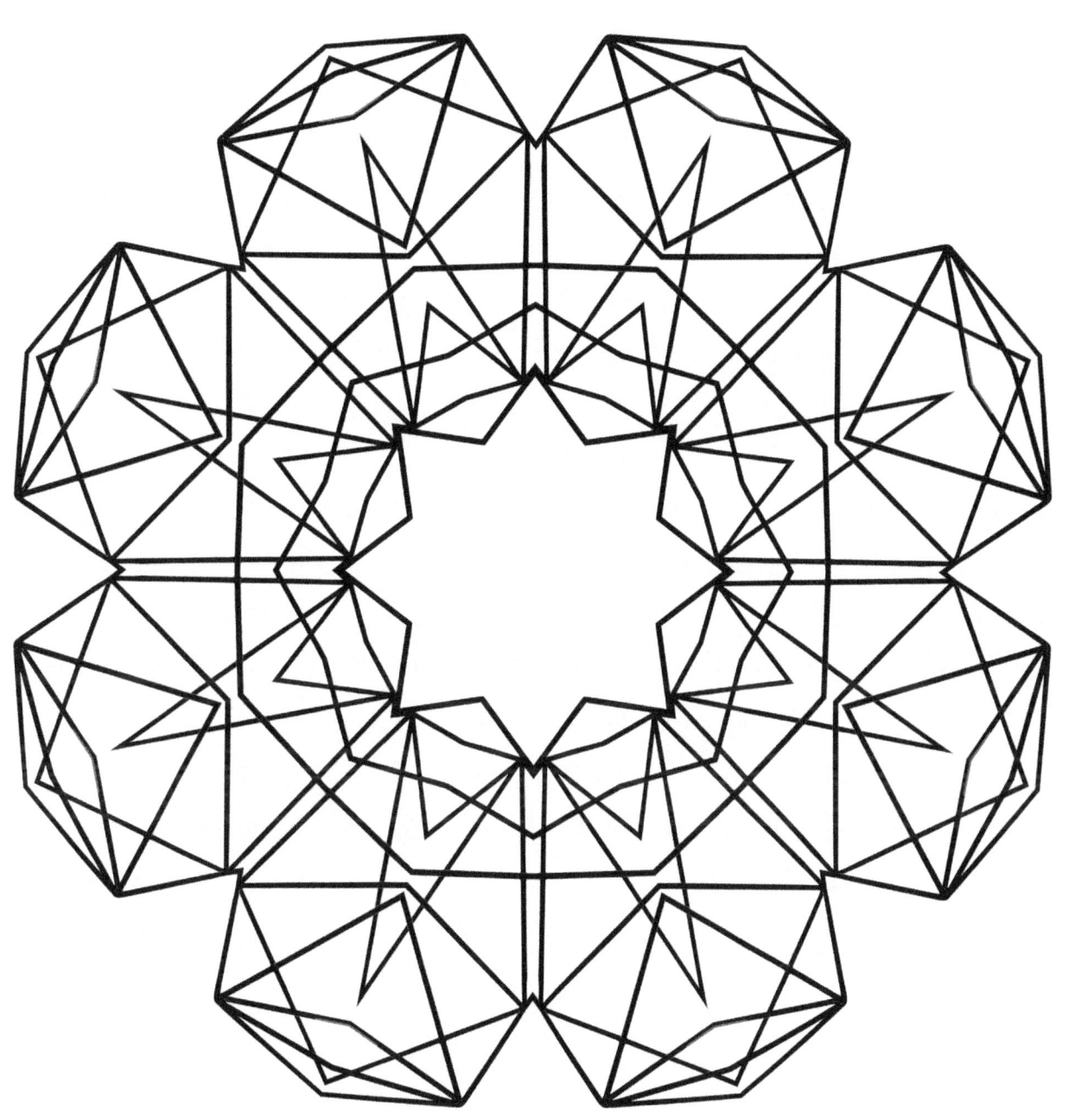

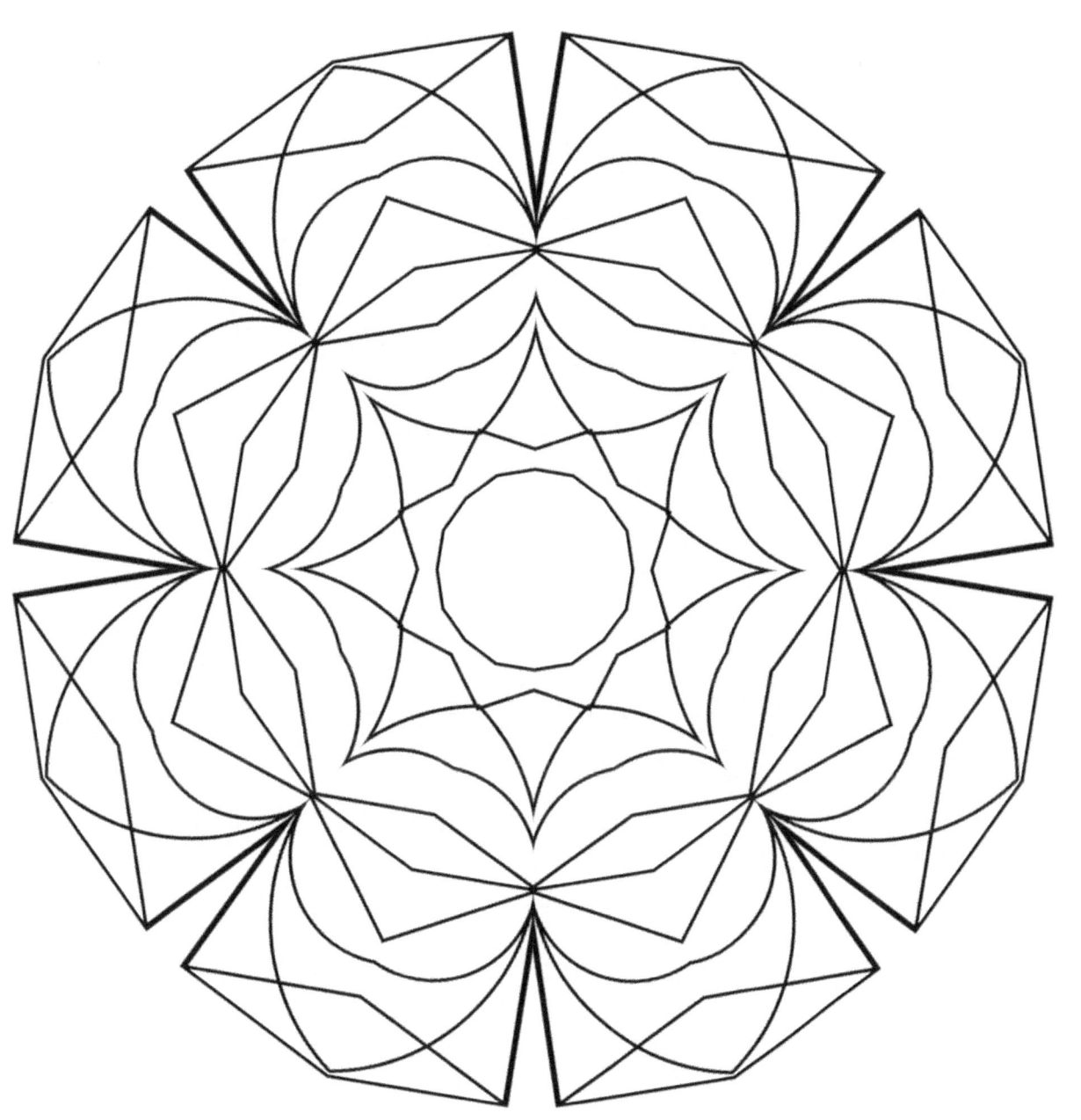

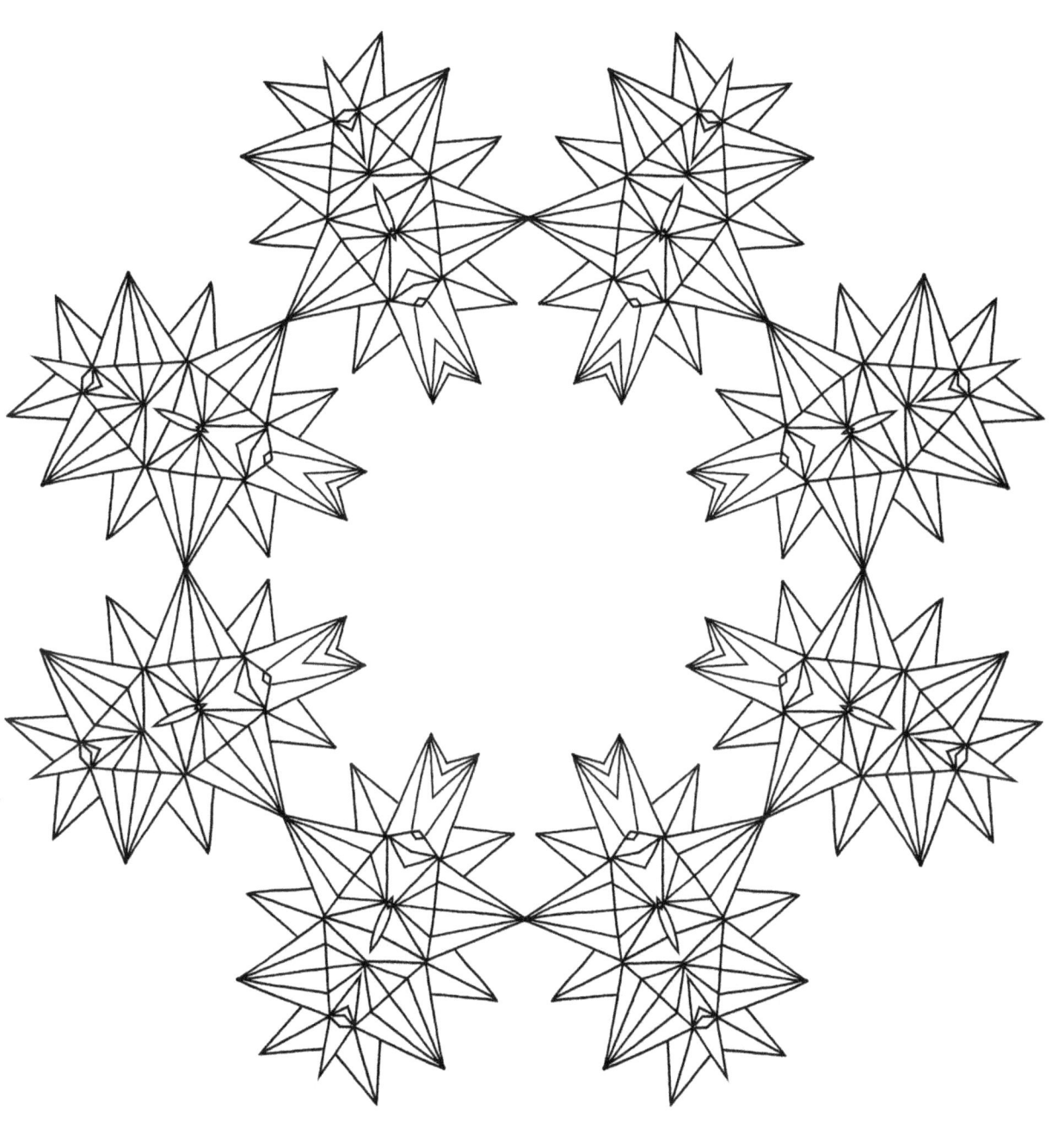

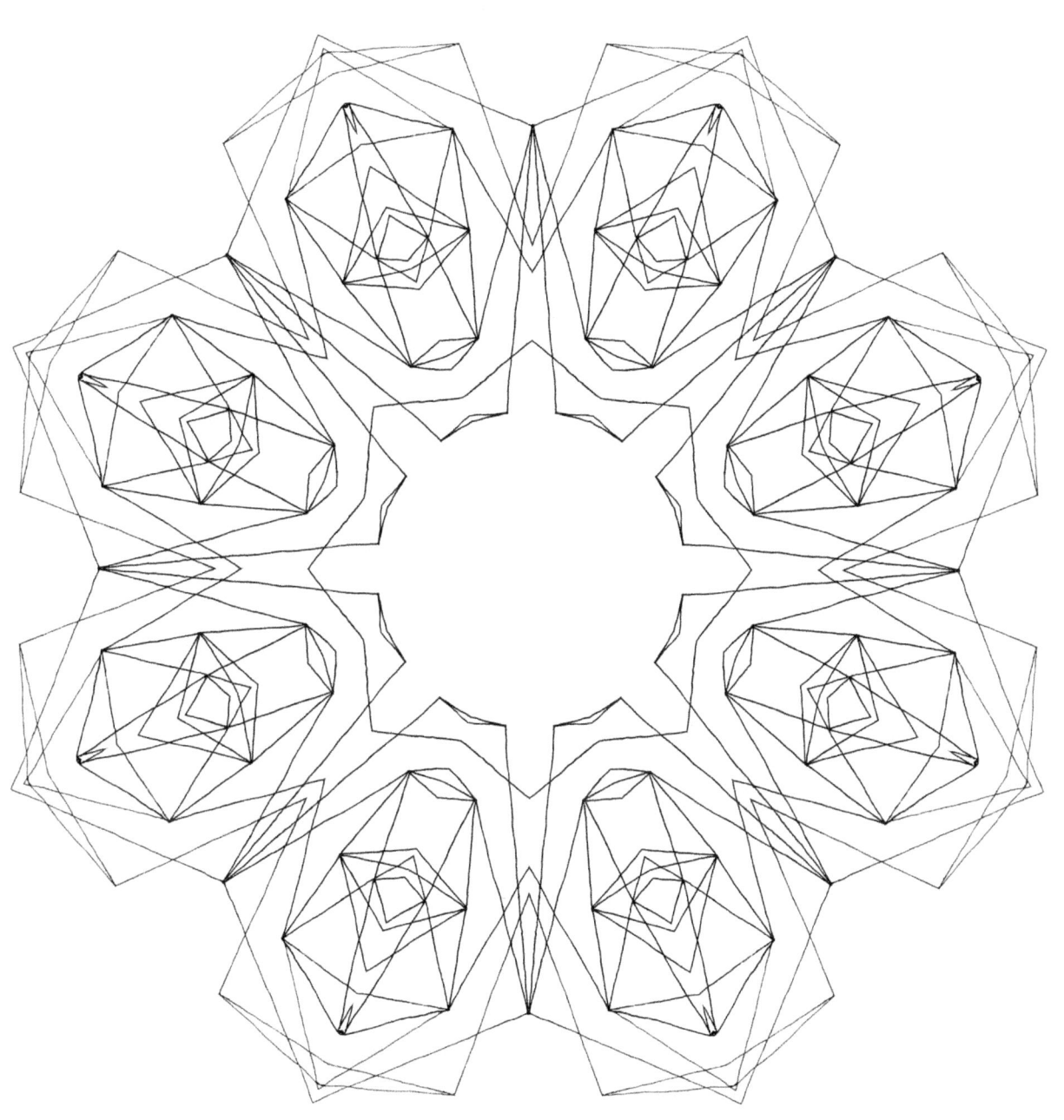

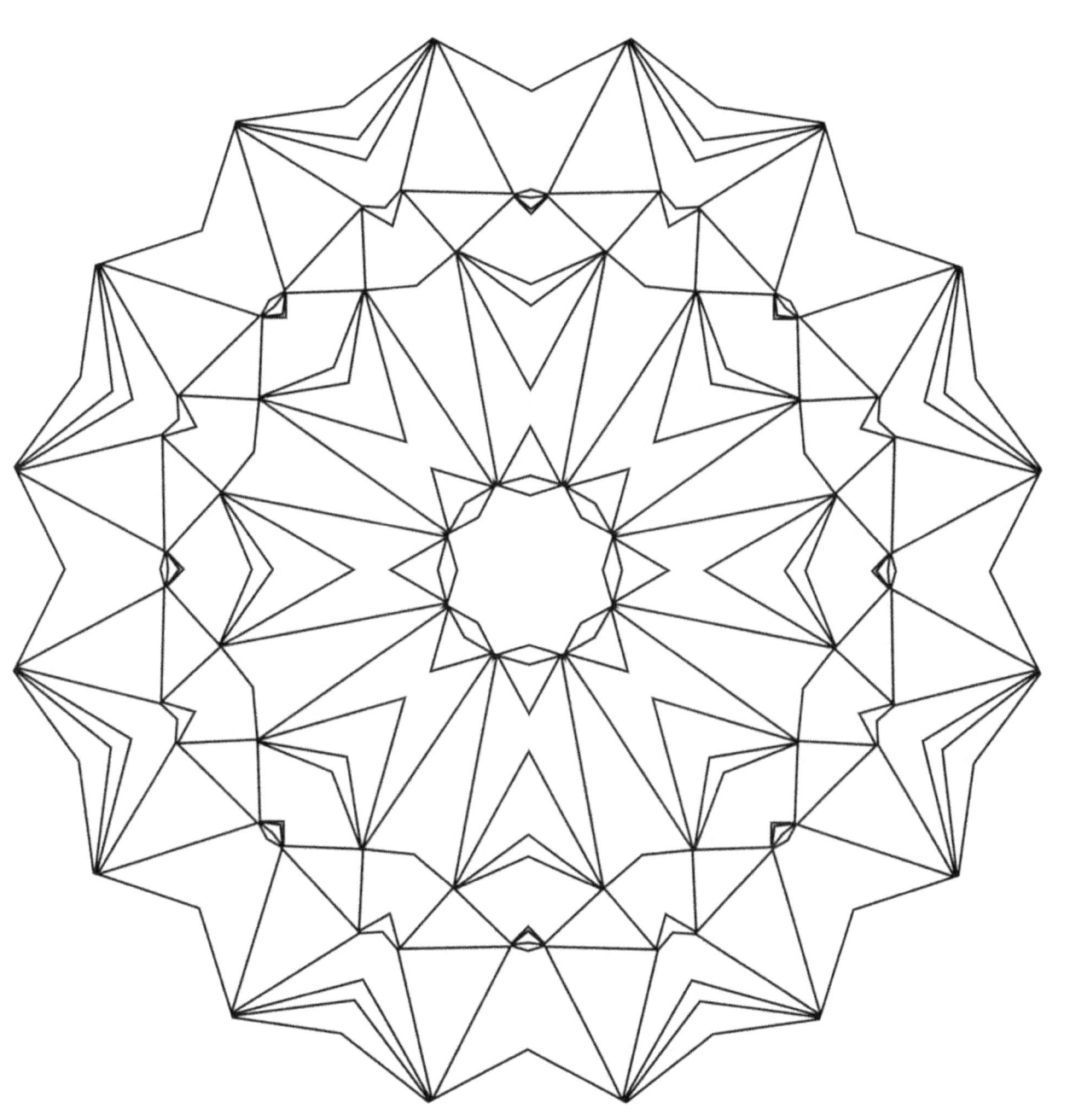

www.ingramcontent.com/pod-product-compliance
Lightning Source LLC
Chambersburg PA
CBHW080709190526
45169CB00006B/2306